GOD

God

DATE DUE

JUN 1 0 1998		
JUN 2 5 1998		

DEMCO 38-297

THE   PILGRIM   LIBRARY
OF   WORLD   RELIGIONS

GOD

EDITED BY JACOB NEUSNER

The Pilgrim Press
Cleveland, Ohio

#36330807

The Pilgrim Press, Cleveland, Ohio 44115
© 1997 by Jacob Neusner

Printed in the United States of America on acid-free paper

02   01   00   99   98   97   5   4   3   2   1

Library of Congress Cataloging-in-Publication Data

God / edited by Jacob Neusner.
        p.   cm. — (The Pilgrim library of world religions ; v. 1)
        Includes bibliographical references and index.
        ISBN 0-8298-1177-X (pbk. : alk. paper)
        1. God—Comparative studies.   2. Religions.   I. Neusner, Jacob, 1932–   .
II. Series.
BL205.G62   1997
291.2'11—dc21   97-210 ·
                                                                          CIP

CONTENTS

T he great world religions address certain existential issues in common, for the human situation raises compelling questions. These questions transcend the limits of time, space, and circumstance, and they speak to the condition of all humanity. On that basis we may listen to the viewpoint on an issue that we confront set forth by a religion we hold, alongside the one maintained by the religion that we do not hold. The purpose of this library can be defined as introducing, comparing, and contrasting the positions of five great world religions on a program of issues they address in common.

Recognizing that each religion forms a system with its own definitive traits, we aver that all religions must and do treat in common a range of fundamental topics as well, and we hold that comparison and contrast among religions begins in the treatment of urgent questions that all of them must resolve. This library introduces the religions of the world as they meet in conversation upon the profound issues of world order, transcendent, individual and familial, and social. In the first rubric falls how we know God; in the second, our life of suffering and death, women, and the aspiration for afterlife; and in the third, the authority and continuity of tradition itself. Indeed, for the purpose of these volumes we may define religion as a theory of the social order that addresses from the unique perspective of transcendence (God, in concrete language) issues of the human condition of home and family, on the one side, and of the public interest, on the other.

The five topics of the initial account require only brief clarification. Common to the human condition is the quest for

God. Everyone suffers and everyone dies. One half of humanity is comprised of women. Humanity everywhere aspires to explain what happens after we die. And, finally, every religion identifies authoritative teaching ("sacred texts"), though what the various religions mean by "a text" will vary, since a person or a drama or a dance as much as a piece of writing may form a fixed and official statement for amplification and exegesis through time. In these five volumes, the initial set in the Pilgrim Library of World Religions, we take up the five topics we deem both critical and ubiquitous in the religions we identify as paramount. Following a single outline, worked out in common, we spell out how each religion addresses the topic at hand. In this way we propose to make possible a labor of comparison of religions: how all address a single issue, uniformly defined.

The religions are chosen because all of them not only speak to humanity in common but also relate in concrete, historical ways. Judaism, Christianity, and Islam join together in a common doctrine, the unity of God, and in valuing a common Scripture, the Hebrew Scriptures of ancient Israel that Judaism knows as the written Torah, which is the Old Testament of Christianity, joined in the case of Christianity and Islam into the Bible, the book, comprising the Old and New Testaments. Hinduism forms the matrix out of which Buddhism took shape, much as ancient Israelite Scriptures amplified by the Judaism of the day defined the matrix in which Christianity originated. Not only do Judaism, Christianity, and Islam conduct an ongoing dialogue between and among themselves, but Christianity and Islam compete in Africa, Hinduism and Islam in India, and Christianity and Buddhism in Southeast Asia and parts of China and Japan. All five religions not only address humanity but reach across the boundaries of ethnic groups and local societies and speak of the condition of humanity. And all five come to formulation in a set of writings deemed classical and authoritative.

That fact—that each of the religions treated here identifies a canon that defines the faith—makes the work possible. For each of the religions treated here proves diverse; viewed over time, all of them yield marks of historical change and diversity of doctrine and practice alike. Take Judaism, for example. Today it breaks down in a number of distinct religious systems or Judaisms, Reform, Orthodox, Conservative, in North America, for instance. Christianity yields three vast divisions, Catholic, Protestant, and Orthodox. The world has gotten to know some of the differences between Shiite and Sunni Islam. Recognizing the Hinayana and Mahayana types of Buddhism, coming to grips with the great diversity of Indian religious communities treated collectively as "Hinduism"—here too we confront the variety of the religious systems that we tend to treat as cogent and collective. And that explains the stress upon the classical as against the contemporary, the initial as against the developed, positions that we outline. The upshot is that while we recognize the density and diversity of each of the religions under study in these volumes, our account of their principal doctrines on critical and universal issues appeals only to those writings that all forms or versions of the several religions acknowledge, to which all Judaisms or Christianities, for instance, will appeal.

That same fact—the appeal to authoritative writings of a classical character—also permits us to describe without nuance of context or historical circumstance the positions of the five religions. To the writings cited here all Judaisms, Christianities, Islams, Buddhisms, and Hinduisms appeal, each in its own framework. People who practice the religions set forth here may believe diverse things within the framework of those religions, respectively; Catholics may practice birth control, for example. So too, religions that bear a distinctive relationship to a given ethnic group—Judaism to Jews, for instance—cannot be defined merely by public-opinion polling of that ethnic group. Not all Jews practice Judaism, and not all Arabs, Islam, nor all

Italians, Catholicism. By concentrating on the classical statements of the religions at hand, we set forth an ideal type, the
picture of the religion that its authoritative writings provide,
not the picture of the religion that the workaday world may
yield.

The same consideration affects the diversity over time and
in contemporary life of the several religions before us. Everyone
understands that all five religions not only produced diverse
systems but also developed and changed over history, so that a
doctrine or belief on a given topic in one time and place may
not conform to the shape of the same doctrine or belief on the
same topic in a different setting. Ideas about God vary, for instance, depending on the situation of the interpreter, learned or
mystic or simple, for instance, or on the age in which the idea is
explained. That is quite natural, given the vast stretches of time
and space traversed by the five religions we examine. While acknowledging the variations produced by the passage of time
and the movement of culture, we appeal to the classical writings
for an account that all later generations of the faithful, wherever
located, can affirm, however diverse the interpretations placed
upon that account. In the section following this preface, Literary Sources of the World Religions, each of the writers lists the
documents that form the foundation of his or her chapter in
this volume.

The Pilgrim Library of World Religions took shape in the
shared intellectual adventure that joins us together as professors
of the academic study of religion at Bard College and in dialogue with our students there. We tried out the various chapters
on them. The chapters were outlined in common. The writers
of the substantive chapters further invited William Scott
Green, University of Rochester, to read and introduce their discussions and to write conclusions, spelling out the results of
putting side by side systematic accounts of how the five reli-

gions respond to exactly the same set of questions. Our respect for his intellectual leadership in the academic study of religion is amply vindicated in the result.

All of us express our appreciation to the president of Bard College, Dr. Leon Botstein, and the dean of faculty, Stuart Levine, for their encouragement of this project; and to Richard Brown, formerly of Pilgrim Press, our patient and gentle editor, whose good ideas always made the work still more challenging and stimulating than our joint venture had made it to begin with.

As distinguished research professor of religious studies at the University of South Florida, the editor enjoys support for all his academic ventures, including permission to devote part of a semester each year to teaching students, also, at Bard College. In this way as a teacher he enjoys the best of both worlds—small liberal arts college, residential and select, and huge state university, with open admissions to an enormous commuting student body, nearly all of it employed in jobs as well as in learning. Each setting presents its challenges and opportunities, and both of them offer unique points of enjoyment and satisfaction as well.

Jacob Neusner
SERIES EDITOR

CONTRIBUTORS

JONATHAN BROCKOPP received his Ph.D. from Yale University and is assistant professor of religion at Bard College.

BRUCE CHILTON is chairman of the Department of Religion, Bernard Iddings Bell Professor of Religion, and chaplain of Bard College.

BRADLEY S. CLOUGH is a Ph.D. candidate at Columbia University and is visiting assistant professor of Asian studies and religion at Bard College.

WILLIAM SCOTT GREEN founded the Department of Religion and Classics at the University of Rochester and is now dean of the undergraduate college.

JACOB NEUSNER is distinguished research professor of religious studies at the University of South Florida and professor of religion at Bard College.

LAURIE PATTON received her Ph.D. from the University of Chicago and is assistant professor of religion at Emory University.

The Pilgrim Press is a leading publisher in Christian ethics and theology. Through the Pilgrim Library of World Religions series, edited by Jacob Neusner, we seek to continue and expand this heritage.

Part of this heritage is a policy regarding the use of inclusive language for human beings and for God. With few exceptions, the Pilgrim Library of World Religions maintains this heritage. Nevertheless we recognize that various religious traditions have struggled differently with inclusive language for God. Therefore each contributor, especially when discussing God's self-revelation, has been offered some flexibility in order to faithfully reflect that religious tradition's current form of expression.

JUDAISM

Judaism, the religion, identifies as its authoritative source "the Torah," or "the teaching," defined as God's revelation to Moses at Sinai. Writings deemed canonical enter the category of Torah, though into that same category also fall all authentic teachings of every age. The revelation myth of Judaism maintains that at Sinai God revealed the Torah in two media, written and oral. That is to say, while part of the revelation took written form, another part was formulated orally and transmitted through memorization. The tradition of Sinai may then come to concrete expression through any great sage's teaching. But the account of the position of Judaism set forth in these pages derives from the dual Torah, written and oral, as set forth in the Hebrew Scriptures and as interpreted by "our sages of blessed memory," the rabbis of the first seven centuries of the common era.

The Written Part of the Torah

We know the written part of the Torah as the Hebrew Scriptures of ancient Israel, or the "Old Testament." This is made up of the Pentateuch, or Five Books of Moses (Genesis, Exodus, Leviticus, Numbers, and Deuteronomy); the Former Prophets (Joshua, Judges, Samuel, and Kings); the Latter Prophets (Isaiah, Jeremiah, and Ezekiel); the Twelve Minor Prophets; and the Writings (Psalms, Proverbs, Job, Song of Songs [aka the Song of Solomon], Ruth, Lamentations, Ecclesiastes, Esther, Daniel, Ezra, Nehemiah, and Chronicles). All translations from the written Torah come from the Revised Standard Version of the Bible.

The Oral Part of the Torah:
The Mishnah, Tosefta, and Two Talmuds
Judaism identifies a philosophical law code called the Mishnah
(c. 200 C.E.) as the first and most important of the finally tran-
scribed components of the oral Torah. The Mishnah is a set of
rules in six parts, made up of laws dealing with the hierarchical
classification of holy Israel in these categories: (1) agricultural
life; (2) the holy calendar, Sabbaths, and festivals; (3) women
and family; (4) civil law and the administration of justice and
the state; (5) the Temple and its offerings; (6) purity laws. A
tractate, or compilation of teachings, called Abot, "the Fathers," attached to the Mishnah, commences, "Moses received
Torah at Sinai and handed it on to Joshua, Joshua to elders, and
elders to prophets. And prophets handed it on to the men of
the great assembly," and onward down to the very authorities of
the Mishnah itself. That is how the document is placed within
the oral tradition of Sinai. In addition to the Mishnah, three
other writings carry forward the legal tradition of Sinai: the
Tosefta (c. 300 C.E.), a set of further legal traditions in the
model of those in the Mishnah; the Talmud of the Land of Israel (c. 400 C.E.), a systematic amplification of thirty-nine of
the Mishnah's sixty-two topical tractates; and the Talmud of
Babylonia (c. 600 C.E.), a commentary to thirty-seven of the
same. The two Talmuds treat in common the second, third,
and fourth divisions of the Mishnah. The former takes up the
first; the latter, the fifth; and neither addresses the sixth. In addition, tractate Abot receives its Talmud in a compilation, the
Fathers according to Rabbi Nathan, of indeterminate date.

The Oral Part of the Torah: Midrash-Compilations
The work of commenting on the Mishnah and its legal traditions found its counterpart, among the same sages or rabbis, in
the labor of commenting on books of the written Torah. This
work produced Midrash, or exegesis, meaning the interpreta-

tion of Scripture in light of contemporary events by appeal to a particular paradigm, or pattern, that showed how Scripture imposed meaning on contemporary occasions. Those biblical books selected for intensive amplification are the ones read in the synagogue: Genesis, in Genesis Rabbah (c. 400 C.E.); Exodus, in Mekhilta Attributed to Rabbi Ishmael (of indeterminate date but possibly in c. 350 C.E.); Leviticus, in Sifra (c. 350 C.E.), and also in Leviticus Rabbah (c. 450 C.E.); Numbers, in Sifré to Numbers; and Deuteronomy, in Sifré to Deuteronomy (both c. 350 C.E.). In addition, Midrash-compilations serve four of the scrolls read in synagogue worship: Lamentations, read on the 9th of Ab to commemorate the destruction of the Temple; Esther, read on Purim; Song of Songs, read on Passover; and Ruth, read on Pentecost. The Mishnah, Tosefta, Talmuds, and Midrash-compilations all together form the authoritative canon of Judaism in its formative age, the first seven centuries of the common era. All translations of portions of the oral Torah come from those made by the author.

CHRISTIANITY

The Christian faith understands itself to be grounded in the Holy Spirit, God's self-communication. Access to the Holy Spirit is possible because in Jesus Christ God became human. The Incarnation (God becoming flesh, *caro* in Latin) is what provides the possibility of the Divine Spirit becoming accessible to the human spirit.

Speaking from the perspective of Christian faith, then, there is a single source of theology: the Holy Spirit, which comes from the Father and Son. But the inspiration of the Holy Spirit has been discovered and articulated by means of distinct kinds of literature in the history of the church. By becoming aware of the diversity of those sources, we can appreciate both the variety and the coherence of Christianity.

The Scriptures of Israel have always been valued within the

church, both in Hebrew and in the Greek translation used in the Mediterranean world. (The Greek rendering is called the Septuagint, after the seventy translators who were said to have produced it.) Those were the only scriptures of the church in its primitive phase, when the New Testament was being composed. In their meetings of prayer and worship, followers of Jesus saw the Scriptures of Israel as "fulfilled" by their faith: their conviction was that the same Spirit of God which was active in the prophets was, through Christ, available to them.

The New Testament was produced in primitive communities of Christians to prepare people for baptism, to order worship, to resolve disputes, to encourage faith, and for like purposes. As a whole, it is a collective document of primitive Christianity. Its purpose is to call out and order true Israel in response to the triumphant news of Jesus' preaching, activity, death, and resurrection. The New Testament provides the means of accessing the Spirit spoken of in the Scriptures of Israel. Once the New Testament was formed, it was natural to refer to the Scriptures of Israel as the "Old Testament."

The Old Testament is classic for Christians because it represents the ways in which God's Spirit might be known. At the same time, the New Testament is normative: it sets out how we actually appropriate the Spirit of God, which is also the Spirit of Christ. That is why the Bible as a whole is accorded a place of absolute privilege in the Christian tradition: it is the literary source from which we know both how the Spirit of God has been known and how we can appropriate it.

Early Christianity (between the second and the fourth centuries of the common era) designates the period during which the church founded theology on the basis of the Scriptures of the Old and New Testaments. Although Christians were under extreme—sometimes violent—pressure from the Roman Empire, Early Christianity was a time of unique creativity. From thinkers as different from one another as Bishop Irenaeus in France and

Origen, the speculative teacher active first in Egypt and then in Palestine, a commonly Christian philosophy began to emerge. Early Christianity might also be called a "catholic" phase, in the sense that it was a quest for a "general" or "universal" account of the faith, but that designation may lead to confusion with Roman Catholicism at a later stage, and is avoided here.

After the Roman Empire itself embraced Christianity in the fourth century, the church was in a position formally to articulate its understanding of the faith by means of common standards. During this period of Orthodox Christianity, correct norms of worship, baptism, creeds, biblical texts, and doctrines were established. From Augustine in the West to Gregory of Nyssa in the East, Christianity for the first and only time in its history approached being truly ecumenical.

The collapse of Rome under the barbarian invasions in the West broke the unity of the church. Although the East remained wedded to the forms of Orthodoxy (and accepts them to this day), the West developed its own structure of governance and its own theology, especially after Charlemagne was crowned as Emperor of the Romans by Pope Leo III on Christmas Day in 800 C.E. European Christianity flourished during the Middle Ages, and Scholastic theology was a result of that success.

The Scholastics were organized on the basis of educational centers, Thomas Aquinas at the University of Paris during the thirteenth century being the best example. During the periods of Early Christianity and Orthodoxy, theologies as well as forms of discipline and worship were developed for the first time. Scholastic theology was in the position of systematizing these developments for the usage of the West. At the same time, Scholastic theologians also rose to the challenge of explaining Christian faith in the terms of the new philosophical movements they came into contact with.

The Reformation, between the sixteenth and the eighteenth centuries, challenged the very idea of a single system of Christianity. Martin Luther imagined that each region might settle on its own form of religion. In England the settlement was on a national basis, while in John Calvin's Geneva the elders of the city made that determination. But in all its variety, the Reformation insisted that the Bible and worship should be put into the language of the people, and that their governance should be consistent with their own understanding of the faith.

From the eighteenth century until the present, Christianity in its modern form has been wrestling with the consequences of the rise of rationalism and science. The results have been diverse and surprising. They include Protestant Fundamentalism—a claim that the Bible articulates certain "fundamentals," which govern human existence—and the Roman Catholic idea of papal infallibility, the claim that the pope may speak the truth of the church without error. In both cases, the attempt is made to establish an axiom of reason that reason itself may not challenge. But modern Christianity also includes a vigorous acceptance of the primacy of individual judgment in the life of communities: examples include the Confessing Church in Germany, which opposed the Third Reich, and the current movement of Liberation Theology in Central and South America.

Today Christians may use many combinations of the sort of sources named here to articulate their beliefs, and the resulting pattern is likely to be as distinctive as what has been produced in the past.

ISLAM

The Qur'ān

The single source that constitutes the basis of all inquiry into the religion of Islam is the Qur'ān. Revealed to the prophet Muḥammad from 610 to 632 C.E., it is understood as God's own speech. That is to say, Muslims believe that the Qur'ān is not merely inspired by God, it is exactly what God meant to say to the early Muslim community and to the world in general. Furthermore, God spoke to Muḥammad (usually through the angel Gabriel) in Arabic, and to this day Muslims resist translation of the Qur'ān into any other language. The Qur'ān is about as long as the Christian New Testament. It is divided into 114 chapters (called *suras*), which range in size from a few verses to a few hundred. All but one of these suras begin with an invocation, "In the name of God, the Merciful, the Compassionate," and with these words pious Muslims begin all endeavors of importance. There are many translations of the Qur'ān into English; that of A. J. Arberry[1] is widely recognized as the best and will be used in this series, despite the unfortunate gender bias in Arberry's language.

The Qur'ān describes itself as a continuation and perfection of a tradition of revelation that began with the Torah, revealed to the Jews, and the Gospels, revealed to the Christians. In fact, the Qur'ān directly addresses Jews and Christians, urging them to put aside their differences and join Muslims in the worship of the one, true God: "Say: People of the Book! Come now to a word common between us and you, that we serve none but God" (The House of Imran, 3:56). Jesus and Moses are explicitly recognized as prophets, and the rules and pious regulations in the Qur'ān fit in well with similar rules found in Judaism and Christianity. Of course, a special role is given to Muḥammad, the seal of the prophets and the leader of the early Muslim community.

Sunna: The Prophet as Text
The prophet Muḥammad serves as the second "text" for Muslims. Unlike the Qur'ān, which is the single source for God's divine word in Islam, the words and deeds of the Prophet are found in many different sources. When it comes to the Prophet, precise words are not as important as his general "way of doing things"; in Arabic, this is called the Prophet's *sunna.* The prophet Muḥammad ibn 'Abd Allāh was born almost six centuries after Jesus' birth, around 570 C.E., and for the first forty years of his

life he organized trading caravans. Around the year 610, he began meditating in a cave near his hometown of Mecca, when he
was overwhelmed by a vision of the angel Gabriel commanding
him, "Recite!" This event changed his life forever and he began,
slowly, to preach to his relatives and neighbors. After years of
effort, Muḥammad and a small group of followers moved to the
town of Medina. This *hijrah*, the emigration of Muslims from
Mecca to Medina in 622 C.E., marks the beginning of the Muslim calendar and was a turning point for the early community.
In Medina, hundreds flocked to the new religion, and when the
Prophet died in 632, he left behind thousands of believers. The
survival of this early group is testified to by the almost one billion Muslims in the world today. Now, as then, Muslims see the
Prophet as an example of the ideal believer. Muslims often name
their boys after the Prophet, wear clothes like his, and try to live
according to his precepts.

Hadith: Examples of the Prophet's Sunna
Muḥammad's words and deeds were preserved and passed on
from generation to generation in a form of oral transmission
known as hadith. The Arabic word *ḥadīth* means "story," and a
typical hadith begins with a list of those from whom the story
was received, going back in time to the Prophet. Following this
list is the story itself, often an account of the Prophet's actions in
a particular situation or the Prophet's advice on a certain problem. The list of transmitters is an integral part of the hadith; for
example: "al-Qāsim—'Ā'ishah—The Prophet said . . ." Here,
al-Qāsim (an early legal scholar) transmitted this hadith from
'Ā'ishah (one of the Prophet's wives), who heard it directly from
the Prophet. These stories were quite popular among early generations of Muslims, but no one attempted to collect and orga-
nize them until over a hundred years after the Prophet's death.
Two important early collections of hadith are those by al-
Bukhārī (d. 870) and Muslim ibn al-Ḥajjāj (d. 875). Hadith are

also found in works of history and in commentaries on the Qur'ān. It is worth emphasizing that Muslims do not believe that Muḥammad was divine. A careful distinction was maintained between divine words, which originated with God and therefore were put into the Qur'ān, and Muḥammad's general advice to his community. Both sets of words were spoken by the Prophet, but the first were written down and carefully preserved, while the second were handed down through the more informal vehicle of hadith.

Tafsīr: Commentary on the Texts

Today, as in previous ages, Muslims often turn directly to the Qur'ān and hadith for guidance and inspiration, but just as often, they turn to commentaries and interpretations of these primary sources. These commentaries concern themselves with questions of grammar, context, and the legal and mystical implications of the text. They expand the original source, often collecting interpretations of many previous generations together. The results can be massive. The Qur'ān, for instance, is only one volume, but a typical commentary can be twenty volumes or more. The importance of commentary in the Islamic tradition demonstrates that the Qur'ān and Sunna of the Prophet are not the only sources for guidance in Islam. Rather, Muslims have depended on learned men and women to interpret the divine sources and add their own teachings to this tradition. Therefore, these commentaries are valuable sources for understanding the religious beliefs of Muslims throughout the ages. Together with the Qur'ān and hadith, they provide a continuous expression of Islamic religious writing from scholars, mystics, and theologians from over fourteen centuries.

BUDDHISM

Upon examining the major bodies of sacred literature in Buddhism, it must first be noted that Buddhism does not define

"canon" in the same sense that the Judaic, Christian, and Islamic religions do. First of all, scriptures comprising a Buddhist
canon are not deemed authoritative on the basis of being regarded as an exclusive revelation granted to humans by a
supreme divine being. In principle, the ultimate significance of
a given scriptural text for Buddhists lies less in the source from
whom it comes, or in the literal meanings of its words, than in
its ability to generate an awakening to the true nature of reality.
Texts are principally valued according to their ability to enable
one to engage in practices leading to an enlightened state of
salvific insight, which liberates one from suffering, although
they can also be utilized to serve other vitally important if less
ultimate purposes, such as the cultivation of compassionate
ethics, explication of philosophical issues, and protection from
obstacles to personal well-being. Buddhism is also distinctive in
that it has never established any one body that has functioned
in an equivalent manner to the Rabbinate, Episcopate, or
Caliphate, charged with the determination of a single, fixed,
closed list of authoritative works for the entire tradition. On a
local level, Buddhist canons, based on the hermeneutical standard of privileging the realization of enlightenment over source
and word, have tended to remain open (to varying degrees) to
the inclusion of new scriptures over the course of history.

It should not be concluded that the factors discussed above
have ever substantially limited the amount of sacred literature
produced in Buddhism, or have relegated scripture to a status
less than primary in the religion's history. On the contrary, the
various major Buddhist collections of scripture are extraordi-
narily voluminous in size[2] and have continuously occupied a
most highly revered place in the tradition as primary sources of
teaching. Appeals to a scripture's provenance have indeed
played a momentous role in Buddhist history, with a primary
determinate of a text's canonicity being recognition of it as containing *buddha-vacana,* the "spoken word" of a Buddha, or

enlightened being—usually Siddhartha Gautama, or Shakya-muni Buddha (563–483 B.C.E.)—the Indian founder of the reli-gion. To reiterate, one can be sure that the authority assigned to buddha-vacana is derived in part from its source, but what is of utmost import is its liberating power as an indicator of enlight-ened wisdom.

Insofar as we can determine it, the buddha-vacana, first transmitted shortly after the end of Shakyamuni Buddha's life by his main disciples, at first came to consist of two major sets of texts. The first set is known as Sutras (Sūtras), and it is com-prised of the discourses of the Buddha (or in some cases of his disciples, but with his sanction), relating the events in his past and present lifetimes and his practical and philosophical teach-ings. The second set, known as the Vinaya, presents the ethical discipline and monastic rules that regulate the life of the *sangha,* or community, as they were laid down by the Buddha. Collectively, these two sets form the core of what is known as Dharma, or Buddhist doctrine.

In addition, Buddhist canons include texts that provide fur-ther explanation and guidance in the Dharma, such as com-mentaries on the Sutras and Vinaya, treatises on philosophical topics, and ritual and meditative manuals. Broadly known as Shastra (Śāstra), or exegesis, this type of work derived its au-thority not from being buddha-vacana, but from being au-thored by those scholiasts, philosophers, and meditation masters who came to be regarded by later Buddhists as of the highest accomplishments and explicatory skills. Perhaps the most important genre of Shastra texts is the collections known as Abhidharma ("Further Dharma"), which consist of system-atic analyses and classifications of doctrine composed by scholastic masters as early as 300 years after the Buddha.

Despite general agreement among Buddhist traditions on the principle that the words of a Buddha and the further exege-ses by great masters of philosophy and meditation are what

constitute authority and canonicity, there has also been profound disagreement among these traditions about conceptions
of what a Buddha is and what a Buddha teaches, and in turn
about which masters best explicated the most efficacious and
reliable means to liberation. In addition to such sectarian
differences, various regional and linguistic divisions have contributed to the compilation of a number of separate canons.
Thus, in speaking of the major sources of Buddhism that will
inform these volumes, it is necessary to briefly identify the religion's major sectarian and regional divisions.

The Buddhist world today can be divided according to three
major traditions, each of which traces its origins to developments in India, presently inhabits a more or less definable geo-
graphic region outside India, and subscribes to a distinctive
body of scriptural sources, which the followers regard as the
most authentic version of the Dharma. The Theravada (Ther-
avāda) ("Teaching of the Elders") tradition was the first of the
three to historically form a distinct community (fourth century
C.E.), and today it continues to thrive in the countries of Sri
Lanka, Thailand, Myanmar (Burma), Laos, and Cambodia.
The Theravada corpus of scripture—known as the Tripitaka
("Three Baskets") because of its division into the three sections
of Sutra, Vinaya, and Abhidharma, described above—was ren-
dered into written form in the Pali language by Sri Lankan elders in the first century B.C.E., but its origins are traced back to
a council convened shortly after the end of the Buddha's life in
the early fifth century B.C.E., during which his leading disciples
orally recited the Buddha's words and began committing them
to memory. Theravadins regard their texts as conserving the
Dharma as it was originally taught and practiced by Shakyamuni and his most accomplished followers, who are known as
arhats, or "worthy ones." Their Tripitaka establishes fundamental Buddhist teachings on the nature of suffering, the
selflessness of persons, the impermanence of all phenomena,

and the path of nonviolent ethics and meditation, which leads to liberating wisdom.

The second major Buddhist tradition, which has called itself the Mahayana (Mahāyāna) ("Great Vehicle") because it has seen its teachings as superior to those of the Theravada and the other (now defunct) preceding early Indian schools, developed in the first centuries of the common era in North India and Central Asia, and has long since come to be the predominant form of Buddhism followed in the East Asian countries of China, Korea, Vietnam, and Japan. While the content of the Vinaya and Abhidharma portions of its canon is closely modeled (with notable exceptions) on texts from the earlier Indian schools (which Mahayanists have labeled collectively as Hinayana [Hīnayāna] or "Small Vehicle"), the Mahayana also presented a new, divergent scriptural dispensation in its Sutra literature. Composed originally in Sanskrit, these Mahayana Sutras were said to be a higher form of buddha-vacana, which had been kept from the inferior Hinayana Buddhists, until the capabilities of humans had evolved enough to employ this more difficult, but also more efficacious, Dharma. Popular texts such as the *Perfection of Wisdom, Lotus, Teaching of Vimalakirti, Flower Garland, Descent into Lanka,* and *Pure Land* Sutras promoted a new spiritual ideal, the career of the paragon figure of compassion and insight, the *bodhisattva* ("enlightenment being"). Focusing on the philosophical and practical tenets espoused in these newly emergent Sutras, the great Indian masters of the first millennium of the common era composed explicatory treatises that would come to stand as centerpieces in the Mahayana canons. Most important are the works of the Madhayamika (Mādhayamika), or "Middle Way," school, which expounded on the central idea of *shunyata* (*śūnyatā*), or "emptiness," and those of the Yogacara (Yogācāra) ("Yoga Practice") school, which developed influential theories on the mind and its construction of objective realities. The subsequent history of Mahayana as it was transformed in East Asia is a complex and varied one, but in the long run two practically oriented schools, namely the Pure Land and Meditation (commonly known in the West by its Japanese name, Zen) schools, emerged as the most popular and remain so today. These schools supplement their canons with texts containing the discourses and dialogues of their respective patriarchs.

The third Buddhist tradition to appear on the historical scene, beginning around the sixth century C.E., is the Vajrayana (Vajrayāna) ("Thunderbolt Vehicle"), commonly known as Tantric Buddhism. The Vajrayana survives today in the greater Tibetan cultural areas of Asia, including the Himalayan kingdoms of Sikkim, Nepal, and Bhutan. Tantric Buddhists regard themselves as Mahayanists, and include in their canon all of the major Mahayana texts mentioned above. However, the Vajrayana itself also claimed a new and divergent dispensation of the Buddha's word, in the form of texts called Tantras. While not philosophically innovative, the Tantras offered novel systems of meditative disciplines and ritual practices known as *sādhanas*. Followers of the Vajrayana maintain that the Tantras are the highest and final words of the Buddha, esoterically preserved until the circumstances were right for their exposure to humanity. As the name Vajrayana suggests, the uniqueness of the Tantras lies in their claim to be providing the most powerful and expeditious means of attaining enlightenment. Like their East Asian Mahayana counterparts, Tantric Buddhists also reserve a place of eminence in their canons for the compositions of their most accomplished masters, who are known as *mahāsiddhas,* or "great adepts."

HINDUISM

What we in the twentieth century call Hinduism is in fact a set of religious practices that have developed over two thousand years of Indian history and have a great variety of textual sources. That history begins with the four Vedas—oral compositions of people who called themselves Aryans and who were the ancestors of many of the inhabitants of India today. The term *Veda* means "knowledge," and these four works comprise the accompaniment to Vedic sacrifice—the main form of worship for the early Aryans. Sacrifice usually involved an animal or vegetable offering to one of the many Vedic gods. The first Veda, the Rig Veda (*Ṛg Veda*), is the oldest (c. 1500 B.C.E.), and comprises the mythological hymns of the sacrifice. The second, the Yajur Veda, contains directions on how to conduct the ritual; the third, the Sama Veda (*Sāma Veda*), contains accompanying musical chants. The final Veda, the Atharva Veda, includes hymns for fertility, healing, and other everyday uses in the domestic context, apart from the public sacrifice.

The second set of works important to Hinduism is more philosophical in nature. These works are the Upanishads (*Upaniṣad*s) (c. 900–300 B.C.E.), and consist of speculation about the power behind the sacrifice, called *brahman,* and the nature of the sacrificing self, called *atman (ātman).* The Upanishads also contain the beginnings of a system of belief in reincarnation—more properly called the transmigration of the individual self—through the endless cycle of births, deaths, and sufferings, called *samsara (saṃsāra).* The Upanishadic philosophers believed that the key to liberation from this cycle of suffering was the union between the atman and brahman. Around 200 B.C.E., these initial ideas were developed into an elaborate science of meditation called Yoga, by the philosopher Patañjali. His treatise, the Yoga Sutra (*Yoga Sūtra*), inaugurated the system of Yoga as we know and practice it today.

While the Vedas, Upanishads, and Yoga Sutra reflect the religious practices of the upper strata, or castes, of Indian society, there was very little textual evidence for popular religious practices until the emergence of the epics, the Mahabharata (*Mahābhārata*) and the Ramayana (*Rāmāyaṇa*). The Maha-

bharata is the story of the tragic war between cousins, the Kauravas and the Pandavas (Pāṇḍavas). The Ramayana depicts the
exploits of Rama (Rāma)—a hero said to be the *avatar* (*avatāra*),
or manifestation, of the god Vishnu (Viṣṇu). In rescuing his wife
Sita (Sītā) from the demon Ravana (Rāvaṇa), Rama slays Ravana and rids the world of the evil. Many see these two epics as
the source of popular theology prevalent in India today. They
are the first texts that make extensive mention of the classical
Hindu pantheon—Shiva (Śiva), Vishnu, Brahma (Brahmā),
and Devi (Devī), or the goddess. The Mahabharata is also the
source of the Bhagavad Gita (*Bhagavad Gītā*)—the "Song to
the Lord Krishna," who, in human form, acts as a charioteer
in the war. Particularly in the nineteenth and twentieth centuries, the Bhagavad Gita has inspired much popular devotion
as a Hindu response to the Christian missionary movement.

Near the end of the period of the composition of the epics
(c. 200 C.E.), many kings, especially in North India, began to
patronize these popular deities and build temples to house
them. Such temples had texts called Puranas (Purāṇas) attached
to them; the term *purāṇa* literally means "story of the olden
times." Puranas are encyclopedic compilations that praised the
exploits of particular deities—Vishnu, Shiva, Brahma, and the
Devi, mentioned above. Notoriously difficult to date, the Puranas range from 200 C.E. to 1700 C.E. Another important set of
texts, called Dharma Shastras (*Dharma Śāstras*), emerged at
about this period; these were elaborate law books that codified
daily life according to rules concerned with purity and pollu-
tion. The most famous of these is the Manavadharmashastra
(*Mānava-dharma-śāstra*), or the Laws of Manu. The Puranas
and the Dharma Shastras provide the bulk of the material upon
which the modern Hindu tradition draws, and they originate
in all regions of India.

The wide geographical spread of the Puranas is partly due to
the fact that devotional movements were not exclusive to the

northern Gangetic plain, where the Vedas and Upanishads were composed, but were inspired equally by the South Indian, or Dravidian, civilizations. These devotional movements were called *bhakti*, literally meaning "belonging to." A *bhakta* is someone who "belongs to" a particular god, and has chosen that god for devotion. Beginning in the eighth century C.E., the South Indian bhaktas wrote poetry that became an influential source for Hinduism. The collection of poems by the Tamil saint Nammalvar (Nammāḻvār), the Tiruvaymoli (*Tiruvāymoḻi*), has attained the same canonical status as the Vedas, and is called the Tamil Veda. In addition, the Bengali saint Caitanya inspired a bhakti movement devoted to Krishna (Kṛṣṇa) in the late fifteenth century C.E.; his followers wrote treatises, among them the *Haribhaktirasamrtasindhu* and *Haribhaktivilasa*, that explain the theology and ritual of devotion to Krishna. Many northern and western Indian poets, such as Mirabai (Mīrā Bai)(b. c. 1420 C.E.) and Tukaram (Tukārām) (1608–1649 C.E.), have contributed significantly to the huge corpus of bhakti poetry and theology that Hindus read and recite today.

The final major source for the study of Hinduism is the Vedanta (Vedānta) philosophical tradition, whose development and systematization is attributed to the teacher Shankara (Śaṅkara) in the ninth century C.E. Shankara, and his major successor, Ramanuja (Rāmānuja) (twelfth century C.E.), developed their philosophy through commentaries, called *bhāṣyas*, on the two main texts of Vedānta—the Vedanta Sutras (*Vedanta Sūtras*) and the Brahma Sutras (*Brahma Sūtras*). These texts summarize the doctrine of the Upanishads, mentioned above. In his classic work, Brahmasutrabhashya (*Brahmasūtrabhāṣya*), Shankara argues a philosophy of nonduality (*advaita*). For him, the perceptions of the mind and the senses are simply *avidya* (*avidyā*), ignorance. In ignorance, we perceive a duality between subject and object, self and the source of self. This perception of duality prevents the self (atman) from complete identity with brahman. When complete identity is achieved, however, there is liberation of the self from all ignorance.

These manifold sources—the Vedas, the Upanishads, the epics, the Puranas, the Dharma Shastras, the diverse corpus of bhakti poetry, and Vedanta philosophy—make up the spiritual foundations of Hindu practice today.

I recently was invited to offer the invocation at a school cere-
mony. The audience would be nearly a thousand students,
ranging in age from seven to eighteen, their teachers, trustees,
and guests. Although the school has a nominal Quaker heritage, its students and faculty are now a culturally and religiously diverse group. At first, the assignment seemed simple:
Utter a few lofty thoughts, recite aspirations for the school
community, invoke the deity, and sit down. But as I began to
prepare my assignment, I recognized that even if the first two
parts were straightforward, the third was not.

Invoke the deity?! What would it mean to do that?

Literally, an invocation is a summoning, a conjuring, an en-
treaty. When we offer an invocation, we engage in an act of
communication. We call upon, or call up, a power we regard as
greater than ourselves and ask it to do something for us, to endorse our hopes, to act on our behalf. If you take that notion se-
riously, then offering an invocation anywhere is a daunting
exercise, but to do so on behalf of a mixed audience is beyond
daunting. It probably is impossible.

In a religiously diverse audience, how can you invoke a deity
without leaving someone out? For religions, like languages, are
only effective in particular, never in general. When you invoke
a god, or a goddess, or a combination of the two, you can't call
out "to whom it may concern." The gods don't like impersonal
invitations any more than we do. Invocations depend on knowing the god by name, using the appropriate titles and adjectives,
and making a request with a proper frame of mind and heart. A
broadly popular opinion holds that being religious is a simple

matter of "believing in God." This book shows that view to be naive and oversimplified. The deities of the world's great literate religions are known idiomatically, in languages, behaviors, texts, and attitudes that have been ingrained in cultures for centuries. Only some religious people interact with their gods primarily through "belief." For countless others, dress, food laws, study of texts, and bodily discipline are the ways the gods are encountered and known.

Let us try to get at the matter of religion's particularity in another way. A famous anthropologist, Melford E. Spiro, defined a religion as "an institution consisting of culturally patterned interactions with culturally postulated superhuman beings."[1] Although this definition is controversial with some scholars, it will help us to see the lessons that this book can teach. Let's take the definition apart to see what its pieces mean.

The definition speaks of "superhuman beings." A superhuman being is a being who is more powerful than humans but not necessarily qualitatively different from humans. Superhuman is not the same as supernatural. A superhuman being can do things for you or can say to you, "I want you to do these things or else I will do something to you." The term *superhuman*, as opposed to *supernatural*, allows the definition to include the ideas of various cultures in which dead ancestors are worshiped though they are not thought of as gods (but they are more powerful than humans).

Next, the definition speaks not of random superhuman beings, but of beings who are "culturally postulated." That is a very concise academic way of saying that different cultures advocate, endorse, make sense of, understand different kinds of superhuman beings. For instance, as you can deduce from this book, it does not make sense for people who practice Judaism or Christianity to worship dead ancestors. That is not culturally intelligible to them. But there are cultures in the world in which the kind of being you worship and the kind of being with whom you interact—whom you invoke for blessing—is an ancestor. Likewise, in cultures dominated by Judaism, Christianity, and Islam, polytheism makes no sense. But, as you will read in this book, in the culture out of which Hinduism developed, it made sense for there to be more than one god. The notion of many gods also made sense in ancient Greece and Rome, among other places. Let's use more local examples. In Roman Catholicism, the superhuman beings with whom humans interact can be saints as well as God. No one confuses the saints with God, but it is possible to pray to a saint for assistance or for guidance or wisdom. In some religions, intermediary figures of that sort are culturally not plausible. This does not mean such figures are errors or mistakes. Rather, it means it would not occur to people in some cultures and religions to have such intermediary figures. So, "culturally postulated" is a way of saying you cannot worship a being that everyone in the world you inhabit says doesn't make any sense. There has to be some sort of fit between the values of a given culture and the sorts of beings that people think are superhuman.

What do religious people do with these culturally postulated superhuman beings? They interact with them. And just as the kinds of superhuman beings that exist are conditioned by the cultures from which they spring or in which the people live, so too the ways of interacting with those superhuman beings are conditioned by those cultures. Interaction can mean a range of things. Interaction can be speech or ethics. It can be prayer. Interaction can be anguish or contemplation. It can be obedience. The gods are known through such interaction. When Spiro's definition says "culturally patterned interaction," it means a kind of interaction that people will find plausible and sensible. For example, in our culture it does not make sense for us to imagine humans having sex with God. But in ancient Greece—if you have read any of the ancient Greek myths, you know this is a familiar notion—the gods could impregnate humans and produce people who are half gods and half human. Having sex with a god is a perfectly good kind of interaction, but it is culturally patterned for ancient Greece, not for us. As you will see from the chapters in this book, the communication patterns between humans and the gods shift from religion to religion. In some traditions, the god engages in a personal relationship with a believer and speaks to him or her with words of insight and knowledge. In other traditions, the will of the deity is discerned through the study of divine teachings, but the deity is not expected to communicate directly with human beings.

The invitation to deliver a simple invocation drew me in a practical way into the problem this book raises for students of religion. It is the same problem that Spiro's definition tries to address. In the practice of religion in a diverse society, and in the study of religion in a college or university, there is a tension between the general and the particular. On the one hand, we hold in the West that there is a category—a phenomenon—called "religion" that is a basic and important part of human experience. To understand human experience better, we want to know how "religion" is constructed and how it works. The analogy to language mentioned above helps to show what is at stake here. We also hold that there is a category or phenomenon called "language," which is a basic and important part of human experience. To understand ourselves better, we want to understand how "language" is constructed and how it works. If we did not have the category "language," we might not think—and might not know *how* to think— that French, Swahili, and Arabic are variants of the same phenomenon. Likewise, if we did not have the category "religion," we might not think—and might not know how to think—that Judaism, Hinduism, and Islam belong in the same category. So the focus on the general helps us to see patterns in the particular.

On the other hand, the particular challenges the general. The editor and authors of this book have taken the category "god," and used it as a lens to explore the general category "religion." But "god" is not necessarily a neutral category, one that applies easily to all religions. One of the questions this book raises, then, concerns the adequacy of the category it explores. Do all the particulars spelled out in the various chapters really belong in the same category? Or do they force us to ask fresh questions about the place of "god" in the world's great literate religions? Do all the religions mean the same thing when they speak of what we in the West call "god"? Or do they mean something else? Does deity play the same role in all religions? Is deity equally important in each? What is the relationship between the way human beings interact with their "god" and the way they think about or believe in that god? This book will help readers raise and refine questions like this. As a reader, then, you should allow each chapter to challenge the adequacy of the category "god" as well as to demonstrate it. In the study of religion, the general and the particular are in constant tension and constant dialogue. That is how knowledge advances.

What did I do with my invitation? I declined to invoke. I explained that an invocation in such a setting could only be a provocation to someone, or some god, and that was a risk neither I nor my audience needed to take.

CHAPTER I

Judaism

HOW DO WE KNOW ABOUT GOD?

T he religion that the world calls "Judaism" calls itself "the
Torah." Judaism knows God through the Torah. The
Torah tells the story of God's self-revelation to humanity
through Israel, beginning with Abraham. It is because God
wants to be known and makes it known that we know our Creator through the Torah. This is the teaching of God from Sinai,
written and oral, and it contains that knowledge that God
wishes to impart to humanity. For those who practice Judaism,
the encounter with God takes place in the Torah, hence, in the
study of the Torah. The place and time for meeting God is not
only at prayer, then, but in the holy circle of sage and disciples,
and it is in books that portray God's self-revelation to Moses at
the burning bush (Exod. 3) or in the still, small voice Elijah
heard when he went back to Horeb to find God but discovered
God is not in the storm or fury, that through all time Israel
finds God. In more secular language, Judaism knows God
through God's self-manifestation in the Torah—and otherwise,
so Judaism maintains, there should be no specific, reliable
knowledge of God, Creator of heaven and earth, who reveals
the Torah and who redeems humanity at the end of days.

Judaism is made up of three components: the Torah, oral
and written; Israel the holy people; and God. Israel the holy
people meets God in the Torah at Sinai, when God—not

Moses—proclaims, "The Lord, the Lord! a God compassionate and gracious, slow to anger, abounding in kindness and faithfulness, extending kindness to the thousandth generation, forgiving iniquity, transgression, and sin" (Exod. 34:6). Only in the revelation of the Torah does Israel attain that certain knowledge about God that holy Israel offers humanity.

Does that mean that God is the angry and vengeful God of the Old Testament, as many suppose? The picture of God whom we meet in the Old Testament when read without sages' interpretation and the God whom the Judaic faithful worship in synagogue prayer under the tutelage of the sages of the oral Torah are not quite the same, for the Hebrew Scriptures that Christianity knows as the Old Testament do not exhaust the Judaic doctrine of God. As the account of the sources of Judaism has already made clear, the Torah of Judaism encompasses not only Scripture—the written part of revelation—but also an oral tradition. Only in the whole Torah, written and oral, do we find the complete doctrine of God that Judaism sets forth. In that one whole Torah that is God's self-manifestation to the holy community that God has called into being, called "Israel," God appears as infinitely merciful and loving, passionate as a teenage lover (in Father Andrew Greeley's memorable characterization, which pertains as much to Judaism as to Christianity), whom the Judaic community knows above all by the name "the All-Merciful." God is made manifest to Israel in many ways, but is always one and the same.

Certainly one of the most memorable characterizations presents God as a warrior, but the following passage shows that that presentation is only partial:

"The Lord is a man of war, the Lord is his name" (Exod. 15:3):
　　Why is this stated?
　　Since when he appeared at the sea, it was in the form of a mighty soldier making war, as it is said, "The Lord is a man of war,"

and when he appeared to them at Sinai, it was as an elder, full of mercy, as it is said, "And they saw the God of Israel" (Exod. 24:10),

and when they were redeemed, what does Scripture say? "And the like of the very heaven for clearness" (Exod. 24:10); "I beheld until thrones were placed and one that was ancient of days sat" (Dan. 7:9); "A fiery stream issued" (Dan. 7:10)

[so God took on many forms.] It was, therefore, not to provide the nations of the world with an occasion to claim that there are two dominions in heaven [but that the same God acts in different ways and appears in different forms]

that Scripture says, "The Lord is a man of war, the Lord is his name."

[This then bears the message:] The one in Egypt is the one at the sea, the one in the past is the one in the age to come, the one in this age is the one in the world to come: "See now that I, even I, am he" (Deut. 32:39); "Who has wrought and done it? He who called the generations from the beginning. I the Lord who am the first and with the last I am the same" (Isa. 41:4).

—Mekhilta Attributed to R. Ishmael Shirata, chap. 1, XXIX:2

The main point then is clear: however we know God, in whatever form or aspect, it is always one and the same God.

The supernatural community that calls itself "Israel"—that is, the Judaic equivalent of "the Christian Church" or "the mystical body of Christ"—knows and loves God as the heart and soul of its life. Three times a day the faithful pray—morning, dusk, and after dark—and throughout the day, responding to blessings that cascade over them, faithful Israelites (that is, Jews who practice the religion Judaism) respond with blessings of thanks, for matters as humble as a glass of water, or as remarkable as surviving a car crash. So faithful Israel knows God as intimate friend and companion and never wanders far from God's sight or God's love.

But can God be known through philosophy, particularly

philosophy of religion? People in general suppose that philosophers can prove the existence of God, that nature's plan or history's course points toward a Creator and Savior. But the
specific truths about God that Judaism learns—the ones that
the Torah teaches—come only from God's own self-revelation
in the Torah itself. Philosophy sets forth knowledge of God in
general, that is, the knowledge to be gained by sifting our experience in this world and drawing conclusions from it. Arguments for the existence of God that move from creation to
Creator exemplify how philosophy affords such knowledge.
The written Torah presents its argument in behalf of divine do-
minion from the facts of nature: "Where were you when I laid
the earth's foundations? Speak if you have understanding. Do
you know who decided its dimensions or who measured it with
a knife? Onto what were its bases sunk? Who set its cornerstone
when the morning stars sang together and all the divine beings
shouted for joy?" (Job 38:4–7).

For its part, the oral part of the Torah too offers its argument
in favor of the one true God, Creator of heaven and earth, and
against idolatry by appealing to the facts of nature. In the following story, which amplifies a verse of the book of Genesis, we
hear how the ancient sages of the Torah envisage the patriarch
Abraham as a child, expounding the belief in God and the re-
jection of the gods that inhere in this world's natural phenomena. Here Abraham conducts a polemic against the belief that
God takes the form of idols, or that God is inherent in the mar-
vels of nature. Abraham sets forth the Judaic belief that God
transcends nature, which God has created.

"Haran died in the presence of his father Terah in the land of his
birth, in Ur of the Chaldaeans" (Gen. 11:28):
  Said R. Hiyya [in explanation of how Haran died in his father's presence], "Terah was an idol-manufacturer. Once he went
off on a trip and put Abraham in charge of the store. Someone

would come in and want to buy an idol. He would say to him, "How old are you?"

He said, "Fifty years old."

He said, "Woe to that man, who is fifty years old and is going to bow down to something a day old." So the man would be ashamed and go his way.

One time a woman came in with a bowl of flour, and said to him, "Take this and offer it before them."

He went and took a stick, broke the idols, and put the stick in the hand of the biggest idol.

When his father came back, he said to him, "Why in the world have you been doing these things?"

He said to him, "How can I hide it from you? One time a woman came in with a bowl of flour, and said to me, 'Take this and offer it before them.' Then this idol said, 'I'll eat first,' and that idol said, 'I'll eat first.' One of them, the largest, got up and grabbed the stick and broke the others."

[Terah] said to him, "Why are you making fun of me! Do those idols know anything [that such a thing could possibly happen]?" [Obviously not!]

He said to him, "And should your ears not hear what your mouth is saying?" He took him and handed him over to Nimrod.

He said to him, "Bow down to the fire."

He said to him, "We really should bow down to water, which puts out fire."

He said to him, "Bow down to water."

He said to him, "We really should bow down to the clouds, which bear the water."

He said to him, "Then let's bow down to the clouds."

He said to him, "We really should bow down to the wind, which disperses the clouds."

He said to him, "Then let's bow down to the wind."

He said to him, "We really should bow down to human beings, who can stand up to the wind."

He said to him, "You're just playing word-games with me. Let's bow down to the fire. So now, look, I am going to throw you into the fire, and let your God whom you worship come and save you from the fire."

Now Haran was standing there undecided. He said, "What's the choice? If Abram wins, I'll say I'm on Abram's side, and if Nimrod wins, I'll say I'm on Nimrod's side. [So how can I lose?]"

When Abram went down into the burning furnace and was saved, Nimrod said to him, "On whose side are you?"

He said to him, "Abram's."

They took him and threw him into the fire, and his guts burned up and came out, and he died in the presence of his father.

That is in line with the verse of Scripture: "And Haran died in the presence of his father, Terah" (Gen. 11:28).

—Genesis Rabbah XXXVIII:XIII

This powerful, polemical story makes the simple point that God stands above all of the manifestations of nature, which were deified by pagan religions. Proving that God exists by reason of the facts of the natural world yields generalities. When the psalmist states, "the heavens declare the glory of God, the sky proclaims of God's handiwork" (Ps. 19:2), the self-evidence of the argument from creation is affirmed. But the specific knowledge about God that the Torah provides comes only there.

That is to say, out of the evidence of nature and history, it is clear, the basic truths about God that Judaism sets forth simply do not emerge. That is why the Torah functions for Judaism as Christ Incarnate does for Christianity: the source of most of what we really know about God in this world and in human terms. Judaism sets forth its theology, deriving from the revealed Torah, when it makes a great many quite specific statements about God. For most of what Judaism knows about God it learns in the Torah. For Judaism God is impassioned, caring, loving, just. Nature read by philosophy makes no provision for a passionate God. Nor does the grand movement of history afford a place to the Lord the Warrior at Israel's crossing of the Sea of Reeds, as we have already seen. These statements about God's Providence in no way recapitulate everyday facts of the workaday world.

That is why knowledge of God such as Judaism sets forth in the end cannot derive wholly from arguments resting on this-worldly facts, on the one side, and human reason, on the other. The knowledge of God that Judaism sets forth derives not from humanity's reasoning about what it knows, but from God's making manifest what only God knows—and wants us to know too. And, for Judaism, God's self-manifestation takes place in the Torah. What we know about God we know because God tells us, and through study of the Torah—oral and written—and its tradition of revelation at Sinai of God to Moses, we acquire knowledge of God.

WHAT DO WE KNOW ABOUT GOD?

The Torah's Sages know God in four aspects:

1. Principle, or premise, that is, the one who created the world and gave the Torah;
2. Presence, e.g., supernatural being resident in the Temple and present where two or more persons are engaged in discourse concerning the Torah;
3. Person, e.g., the one to whom prayer is addressed; and
4. Personality, a God we can know and make our model.

When God emerges as a personality, God is (1) represented as corporeal; (2) exhibits traits of emotions like those of human beings; (3) does deeds that women and men do, in the way in which they do them. But in the end, while humanity is like God, God is always God alone. That is to say, the Torah represents God in ways that we can grasp, with physical traits like ours ("in our image, after our likeness"). God feels the way we do. God acts the way we do. But the Torah always represents God as unique and other than human. (Christianity makes a counterpart statement when it speaks of Christ as unique.)

Let us start with the urgent question: What, precisely, does Judaism claim to learn about God in the Torah? The answer presents us with one of the most distinctive traits of the Torah's presentation of knowledge of God. To understand the point, we must begin with the simple conviction that the Torah represents God's message in God's own wording. God gave the Torah in words of God's own choice, and that means, if we study the Torah, we enter into God's own thought-world. For it is through how God states matters, as much as through what God says, that we know God.

Set forth verbatim in God's wording ("God spoke to Moses saying, Speak to the children of Israel and say to them . . .") the Torah shows us how sentences take shape, words form intelligible propositions, as God speaks, and from the sentences we can learn the grammar—moral, metaphysical, theological alike—of God's intellect. In the written part of the Torah Israel finds itself able to master the language of God's mind, the processes of God's thought. In the work of amplification and application of the written part of the Torah that is undertaken in the oral part, Israel tries to speak that very same language, to form part of the conversation. So in the written Torah Israel works its way back from the Torah to God's rationality, from the world to God's purpose and will. In the oral Torah· Israel makes use of the principles of thought that God has exposed.

This view that in the Torah God is made manifest and, in particular, God's modes of thought become known, is expressed in the claim that, when God made the world, God took the Torah, and, with the perspective of the architect, made use of the Torah as a plan in hand at the outset of the building. Then

the Torah, oral and written, affords us perspective on the building—but, in the nature of things, only from inspection of the
finished edifice. Comparing the world to the Torah, and the
Torah to God's plan and intent, and these to the shape and
structure of God's mind, which correspond to ours—these are
the breathtaking conceptions that the Torah itself opens up to
us: what is humanity, indeed, that through the Torah that man-
ifests God we should think like God! The following expresses
the point:

"In the beginning God created" (Gen. 1:1):

R. Oshaia commenced [discourse by citing the following
verse:] "'Then I was beside him like a little child, and I was daily
his delight [rejoicing before him always, rejoicing in his inhabited
world, and delighting in the sons of men]' (Prov. 8:30–31).

"The word for 'child' uses consonants that may also stand for
'teacher,' 'covered over,' and 'hidden away.' . . .

Another matter:

The word means "workman."

[In the cited verse] the Torah speaks, "I was the work-plan of
the Holy One, blessed be he."

In the accepted practice of the world, when a mortal king
builds a palace, he does not build it out of his own head, but he
follows a work-plan.

And [the one who supplies] the work-plan does not build out
of his own head, but he has designs and diagrams, so as to know
how to situate the rooms and the doorways.

Thus the Holy One, blessed be he, consulted the Torah when
he created the world.

So the Torah stated, "By means of 'the beginning' [that is to
say, the Torah] did God create . . ." (Gen. 1:1).

And the word for "beginning" refers only to the Torah, as
Scripture says, "The Lord made me as the beginning of his way"
(Prov. 8:22).   —Genesis Rabbah I:I.1–2

The Torah is the plan, fully in hand; so God created the way a philosopher or architect does, consulting the principles in laying out the lines of the building. God made the Torah so as to know how to make the world. From the world to the mind of the Creator of the world through the close encounter with the plan for creation. True, all that humanity now has for understanding the world as God wants it to be is the Torah. But, seen in light of the remarkably spacious claim at hand, that suffices for the labor at hand.

In creating the Torah, the sage thus maintains, God worked logically. The Torah then, in exposing the logic of God the Creator's intellect, affords access to the inner structure of the world. Then, through study of the Torah, the sage can uncover, out of the details, the plan of the whole—so doing the work of the theologian. Working back from the correspondence of the world to the details of the Torah, guided by the Torah, not the data of the world, we therefore gain access to the plan that guides God: what is in God's own mind, how God's own intellect does its work. And in our context, our very capacity for understanding, for entering into the logic of the world, gives testimony to how our minds correspond to God's. It is in intellect, as much as emotion and attitude, that we can become *like God*: "in our image, after our likeness," as, the creation narrative tells us, we have been created.

Here we find a remarkable hymn of praise to humanity's capacity to think and reason! Our—humanity's—processes of analytical reasoning rightly carried out replicate God's, we can think like God and in that way be holy like God. Why do the rules of rational thinking reveal to our minds the mind of God? It is because God is bound by the same rules of logical analysis and sound discourse that govern sages. That view is not left merely implicit but is stated explicitly as well. In the following story, also found for the first time in the second Talmud and assuredly speaking for its authorship, we find an explicit affirmation of the priority of reasoned argument over all other forms of discovery of truth. The story begins with a dispute among sages about a certain problem, followed by an account of how Heaven followed the debate but in the end respected sages' right to reason things out on their own:

There we have learned: If one cut [a clay oven] into parts and put sand between the parts,

R. Eliezer declares the oven broken-down and therefore insusceptible to uncleanness.

And sages declare it susceptible.

And this is what is meant by the oven of Akhnai [M. Kel. 5:10].

Why [is it called] the oven of Akhnai?

Said R. Judah said Samuel, "It is because they surrounded it with argument as with a snake and proved it was insusceptible to uncleanness."

It has been taught on Tannaite authority [that is, on the authority of the sages responsible for the first documents of the oral Torah to reach transcription, such as the Mishnah]:

On that day R. Eliezer produced all of the arguments in the world, but they did not accept them from him. So he said to them, "If the law accords with my position, this carob tree will prove it."

The carob was uprooted from its place by a hundred cubits— and some say, four hundred cubits.

They said to him, "There is no proof from a carob tree."

So he went and said to them, "If the law accords with my position, let the stream of water prove it."

The stream of water reversed flow.

They said to him, "There is no proof from a stream of water."

So he went and said to them, "If the law accords with my position, let the walls of the school house prove it."

The walls of the school house tilted toward falling.

R. Joshua rebuked them, saying to them, "If disciples of sages

are contending with one another in matters of law, what business
do you have?"

They did not fall on account of the honor owing to R. Joshua,
but they also did not straighten up on account of the honor owing
to R. Eliezer, and to this day they are still tilted.

So he went and said to them, "If the law accords with my position, let the Heaven prove it!"

An echo came forth, saying, "What business have you with R.
Eliezer, for the law accords with his position under all circumstances!"

R. Joshua stood up on his feet and said, "'It is not in heaven'
(Deut. 30:12)."

What is the sense of, "'It is not in heaven' (Deut. 30:12)"?

Said R. Jeremiah, "[The sense of Joshua's statement is this:]
For the Torah has already been given from Mount Sinai, so we do
not pay attention to echoes, since you have already written in the
Torah at Mount Sinai, 'After the majority you are to incline'
(Exod. 23:2)."

The reasoning of the majority of sages governs; and the story
now reaches its climax:

R. Nathan came upon Elijah and said to him, "What did the Holy
One, blessed be he, do at that moment?"

He said to him, "He laughed and said, 'My children have overcome me, my children have overcome me!'"

—Talmud of Babylonia Baba Mesia 59a–b

God respects reason and values rationality, so in the end God
makes the law in accord with a rule of logic that governs God as
much as it governs humanity. And through the Torah, God has
revealed that rationality.

Through the ages, those concluding words have inspired the
disciples of sages at their work: through intelligent argument

the sage may overcome in argument the very Creator of heaven and earth, the One who gives the Torah—and is bound by its rules too. Here, in the Torah, humanity is not only like God but, in context, equal to God because subject to the same logic. In secular terms a corresponding proposition is the conception of theoretical mathematics as the actual description of nature.

But with this difference: the testimony of nature on its own is null. The heavens declare the glory of God—but only because the psalmist says so. "You have seen what I have done," but only because God tells Moses that that is how events add up to meaning. Uninterpreted by the Torah, neither nature nor history without the structure of meaning manifest in the Torah bears compelling messages. Only the Torah does, and the Torah imposes its messages upon nature and history alike.

And the Torah takes its stand against the arbitrary and capricious: God is bound by the same rules of logical argument, of relevant evidence, of principled exchange, as are we. So we can argue with the mere declaration of fact or opinion—even God's, beyond the Torah, must be measured against God's, within the Torah. The (mere) declaration of matters by Heaven is dismissed. Why? Because God is bound by the rules of rationality that govern in human discourse, and because humanity in the person of the sage thinks like God, as God does; so right is right, and nature has no call to intervene, nor even God to reverse the course of rational argument. That is why the Torah forms the possession of sages, and sages master the Torah through logical argument, right reasoning, the give and take of proposition and refutation, argument and counterargument, evidence arrayed in accord with the rules of proper analysis.

What then does Judaism claim to know about God? It is God's rationality, for the Torah is a revelation of reason, and this in two ways: (1) reason itself is encompassed in what is revealed, and (2) through reason the divine imperative is made compelling. Then the majority will be persuaded, one way or the other, entirely by sound argument: and the majority prevails on that account. God is now bound to the rules of rationality that govern the minds of our sages, and if reason or logic compels a given decision, God is compelled too.

God's self-manifestation takes the form not of presence alone ([1] there is a God in the world, and [2] God is one), nor of person alone ([1] the one God hears prayer and answers, [2] loves us and accords us grace), but of intellectual incarnation: we are like God in the shared, self-evident rules of utter rationality. God has revealed these in the Torah, and in them we encounter God's own intellect. The theology of Judaism sets forth, out of that medium of self-revelation in the Torah itself, God's will and intellect.

Now to return to our starting point on what Judaism knows about God. As we saw, the oral Torah portrays God in four ways: as premise, presence, person, and personality. A definitive statement of the proposition that in diverse forms God appears to humanity is in the following, which represents the state of opinion of the fully exposed religious system of Judaism, at the time of the Talmud of the Land of Israel:

Another interpretation of I am the Lord your God [who brought you out of the land of Egypt] (Exod. 20:2):

Said R. Hinena bar Papa, "The Holy One, blessed be he, had made his appearance to them with a stern face, with a neutral face, with a friendly face, with a happy face.

"with a stern face: in Scripture. When a man teaches his son Torah, he has to teach him in a spirit of awe.

"with a neutral face: in Mishnah.

"with a friendly face: in Talmud.

"with a happy face: in lore.

"Said to them the Holy One, blessed be he, 'Even though you may see all of these diverse faces of mine, nonetheless: I am the Lord your God who brought you out of the land of Egypt' (Exod. 20:2)."

So far we deal with attitudes. As to the iconic representation of God, the following is explicit:

> Said R. Levi, "The Holy One, blessed be he, had appeared to them like an icon that has faces in all directions, so that if a thousand people look at it, it appears to look at them as well.
>
> "So too when the Holy One, blessed be he, when he was speaking, each Israelite would say, 'With me in particular the Word speaks.'
>
> "What is written here is not, I am the Lord, your [plural] God, but rather, I am the Lord your [singular] God who brought you out of the land of Egypt (Exod. 20:2)."

That God may show diverse faces to various people is now established. The reason for God's variety is made explicit. People differ, and God, in the image of whom all mortals are made, must therefore sustain diverse images—all of them formed in the model of human beings. Thus far we should imagine that the Torah's God is a God for intellectuals, scholars, and professors. But that is far from the truth. God is made manifest to each person in accord with his or her capacities and character:

> Said R. Yosé bar Hanina, "And it was in accord with the capacity of each one of them to listen and understand what the Word spoke with him.
>
> "And do not be surprised at this matter, for when the manna came down to Israel, all would find its taste appropriate to their circumstance, infants in accord with their capacity, young people in accord with their capacity, old people in accord with their capacity.
>
> "Infants in accord with their capacity: just as an infant sucks from the teat of his mother, so was its flavor, as it is said, Its taste was like the taste of rich cream (Num. 11:8).
>
> "Young people in accord with their capacity: as it is said, My bread also which I gave you, bread and oil and honey (Ezek. 16:19).

"Old people in accord with their capacity: as it is said, The taste of it was like wafers made with honey (Exod. 16:31).

"Now if in the case of manna, each one would find its taste appropriate to his capacity, so in the matter of the Word, each one understood in accord with capacity.

"Said David, The voice of the Lord is [in accord with one's] in strength (Ps. 29:4).

"What is written is not, in accord with his strength in particular, but rather, in accord with one's strength, meaning, in accord with the capacity of each one.

"Said to them the Holy One, blessed be he, 'It is not in accord with the fact that you hear a great many voices, but you should know that it is I who [speaks to all of you individually]: I am the Lord your God who brought you out of the land of Egypt' (Exod. 20:2)."   —Pesiqta deRab Kahana XII:XXV

The individuality and particularity of God rest upon the diversity of humanity, created "in our image, after our likeness." But, it must follow, the model of humanity—"in our image" dictates how we are to envisage the face of God. And that is the starting point of our inquiry. The Torah defines what we know about God—but the Torah also tells us that we find God in the face of the other: in our image, after our likeness, means everyone is in God's image, so if we want to know God, we had best look closely into the face of all humanity, one by one, one by one.

The Hebrew Scriptures had long ago portrayed God in richly personal terms: God wants, cares, demands, regrets, says and does—just like human beings. In the written Torah God is not merely a collection of abstract theological attributes and thus rules for governance of reality, nor a mere person to be revered and feared. God is not a mere composite of regularities, but a very specific, highly particular personality, whom people can know, envision, engage, persuade, impress. Sages painted this portrait of a personality through making up narratives, telling stories in which God figures like other (incarnate) heroes. When therefore the authorships of documents of the canon of the Judaism of the oral half of the dual Torah began to represent God as personality, not merely premise, presence, or person, they reentered that realm of discourse about God that Scripture had originally laid out.

HOW DO WE RELATE TO GOD?
THE IMITATION OF GOD

For sages God and humanity are indistinguishable in their physical traits. They are distinguished in other, important ways. The issue is the re-presentation of God in the form of humanity, but as God. Let us begin with the conception that God and the human being are mirror images of one another. Here we find the simple claim that the angels could not discern any physical difference whatever between man—Adam—and God:

> Said R. Hoshaiah, "When the Holy One, blessed be he, came to create the first man, the ministering angels mistook him [for God, since man was in God's image,] and wanted to say before the latter, 'Holy, [holy, holy is the Lord of hosts].'
>
> "To what may the matter be compared? To the case of a king and a governor who were set in a chariot, and the provincials wanted to greet the king, 'Sovereign!' But they did not know which one of them was which. What did the king do? He turned the governor out and put him away from the chariot, so that people would know who was king.
>
> "So too when the Holy One, blessed be he, created the first man, the angels mistook him [for God]. What did the Holy One, blessed be he, do? He put him to sleep, so everyone knew that he was a mere man.
>
> "That is in line with the following verse of Scripture: 'Cease you from man, in whose nostrils is a breath, for how little is he to be accounted' (Isa. 2:22)."   —Genesis Rabbah VIII:X

It was in the Talmud of Babylonia—the final, and authoritative, restatement of the whole Torah, oral and written, that emerged from classical times—in particular that God is represented as a fully exposed personality, like man. There we see in a variety of dimensions the single characterization of God as a personality that humanity can know and love.

It becomes possible to relate to God, to imitate God, when God then emerges not as an abstract entity with theological traits but as a fully exposed personality. God is portrayed as engaged in conversation with human beings because God and humanity can understand one another within the same rules of discourse. When we speak of the personality of God, we shall see, traits of a corporeal, emotional, and social character form the repertoire of appropriate characteristics. To begin with, we consider the particular means by which, in the pages of the Talmud of Babylonia, in particular, these traits are set forth. The following story shows us the movement from the abstract and theological to the concrete and narrative mode of discourse about God:

"And Moses made haste and bowed his head toward the earth and worshipped (Exod. 34:8)":

What did Moses see?

Hanina b. Gamula said, "He saw [God's attribute of] being long-suffering [Exod. 34:7]."

Rabbis say, "He saw [the attribute of] truth [Exod. 34:7]." It has been taught on Tannaite authority in accord with him who has said, "He saw God's attribute of being long-suffering."

For it has been taught on Tannaite authority:

When Moses went up on high, he found the Holy One, blessed be he, sitting and writing, "Long-suffering."

He said before him, "Lord of the world, 'Long-suffering for the righteous'?"

He said to him, "Also for the wicked."

[Moses] said to him, "Let the wicked perish."

He said to him, "Now you will see what you want."

When the Israelites sinned, he said to him, "Did I not say to you, 'Long-suffering for the righteous'?"

[Moses] said to him, "Lord of the world, did I not say to you, 'Also for the wicked'?"

That is in line with what is written, "And now I beseech you, let the power of my Lord be great, according as you have spoken, saying" (Num. 14:17). [What called forth Moses' worship of God when Israel sinned through the Golden Calf was his vision of the Almighty as long-suffering.]   —Babli San 111a-b, VI

Once we are told that God is long-suffering, then it is in particular, narrative form that that trait is given definition. Here is one among many answers to those who represent the God of Judaism as vengeful and angry. God then emerges as a personality, specifically because Moses engages in argument with God. He reproaches God, questions God's actions and judgments, holds God to a standard of consistency—and receives appropriate responses. God in heaven does not argue with humanity on earth. God in heaven issues decrees, forms the premise of the earthly rules, constitutes a presence, may even take the form of a "you" for hearing and answering prayers.

When God argues, discusses, defends and explains actions, emerges as a personality etched in words, then God attains that personality that imparts to God the status of a being consubstantial with humanity—that is, of the same substance as us. It is in particular through narrative that that transformation of God from person to personality takes place. Since personality involves physical traits, attitudes of mind, emotion, and intellect consubstantial with those of human beings, and the doing of the deeds people do in the way in which they do them, we shall now see that all three modes of personality come to full expression in the Talmud of Babylonia. This we do in sequence, ending with a clear demonstration that God incarnate takes the particular form of a sage. But no one confuses a sage with God!

God emerges as a fully exposed personality. The character of divinity encompasses God's virtue, the specific traits of character and personality that God exhibited above and here below. Above all, humility, the virtue sages most often asked of themselves, characterizes the divinity. God wanted people to be humble, and God therefore showed humility.

> Said R. Joshua b. Levi, "When Moses came down from before the Holy One, blessed be he, Satan came and asked [God], 'Lord of the world, Where is the Torah? [What have you done with it? Do you really intend to give it to mortals?]'
>
> "He said to him, 'I have given it to the earth . . .' [Satan ultimately was told by God to look for the Torah by finding the son of Amram.]
>
> "He went to Moses and asked him, 'Where is the Torah that the Holy One, blessed be he, gave you?'
>
> "He said to him, 'Who am I that the Holy One, blessed be he, should give me the Torah?'
>
> "Said the Holy One, blessed be he, to Moses, 'Moses, you are a liar!'
>
> "He said to him, 'Lord of the world, you have a treasure in store which you have enjoyed everyday. Shall I keep it to myself?'
>
> "He said to him, 'Moses, since you have acted with humility, it will bear your name: "Remember the Torah of Moses, my servant" (Mal. 3:22).'"   —Talmud of Babylonia Shab 89a

God here is represented as favoring humility and rewarding the humble with honor. What is important is that God does not here cite Scripture or merely paraphrase it; the conversation is an exchange between two vivid personalities. True enough, Moses, not God, is the hero. But the personality of God emerges in vivid ways.

The humanity of God emerges in yet another way. As in the written Torah, so in the oral Torah, the covenant prevails. So God enters into transactions with human beings and accords with the rules that govern those relationships. So God exhibits precisely the social attributes that human beings do. A number of stories, rather protracted and detailed, tell the story of God as a social being, living among and doing business with mortals. These stories provide extended portraits of God's relationships, in particular arguments, with important figures, such as angelic figures, as well as Moses, David, and Hosea. In them God negotiates, persuades, teaches, argues, exchanges reasons. The personality of God therefore comes to expression in a variety of portraits of how God will engage in arguments with men and angels, and so enters into the existence of ordinary people. These disputes, negotiations, transactions yield a portrait of God who is reasonable and capable of give-and-take, as in the following:

> Rabbah bar Mari said, "What is the meaning of this verse: 'But they were rebellious at the sea, even at the Red Sea; nonetheless he saved them for his name's sake' (Ps. 106:7)?
>
> "This teaches that the Israelites were rebellious at that time, saying, 'Just as we will go up on this side, so the Egyptians will go up on the other side.' Said the Holy One, blessed be he, to the angelic prince who reigns over the sea, 'Cast them [the Israelites] out on dry land.'
>
> "He said before him, 'Lord of the world, is there any case of a slave [namely, myself] to whom his master [you] gives a gift [the Israelites], and then the master goes and takes [the gift] away again? [You gave me the Israelites, now you want to take them away and place them on dry land.]'
>
> "He said to him, 'I'll give you one-and-a-half times their number.'
>
> "He said before him, 'Lord of the world, is there a possibility

that a slave can claim anything against his master? [How do I know that you will really do it?]'

"He said to him, 'The Kishon brook will be my pledge [that I shall carry out my word. Nine hundred chariots at the brook were sunk (Judg. 3:23), while Pharaoh at the sea had only six hundred, thus a pledge one-and-a-half times greater than the sum at issue].'

"Forthwith [the angelic prince of the sea] spit them out onto dry land, for it is written, 'And the Israelites saw the Egyptians dead on the seashore' (Exod. 14:30)."

—Talmud of Babylonia Arakhin 15a–b

God is willing to give a pledge to guarantee God's word. God furthermore sees the right claim of the counterpart actor in the story. Hence we see how God obeys precisely the same social laws of exchange and reason that govern other incarnate beings.

Still more interesting is the picture of God's argument with Abraham. God is represented as accepting accountability, by the standards of humanity, for what God does.

Said R. Isaac, "When the Temple was destroyed, the Holy One, blessed be he, found Abraham standing in the Temple. He said to him, 'What is my beloved doing in my house?'

"He said to him, 'I have come because of what is going on with my children.'

"He said to him, 'Your children sinned and have been sent into exile.'

"He said to him, 'But wasn't it by mistake that they sinned?'

"He said to him, 'She has wrought lewdness' (Jer. 11:15).

"He said to him, 'But wasn't it just a minority of them that did it?'

"He said to him, 'It was a majority' (Jer. 11:15).

"He said to him, 'You should at least have taken account of the covenant of circumcision [which should have secured forgiveness despite their sin]!'

"He said to him, 'The holy flesh is passed from you' (Jer. 11:15).

"And if you had waited for them, they might have repented!'

"He said to him, 'When you do evil, then you are happy' (Jer. 11:15).

"He said to him, 'He put his hands on his head, crying out and weeping, saying to them, "God forbid! Perhaps they have no remedy at all!"'

"A heavenly voice came forth and said, 'The Lord called you "a leafy olive tree, fair with excellent fruit"' (Jer. 11:16).

"'Just as in the case of an olive tree, its future comes only at the end [that is, it is only after a long while that it produces its best fruit], so in the case of Israel, their future comes at the end of their time.'"   —Talmud of Babylonia Menahot 53b

God relates to Abraham as to an equal. That is shown by God's implicit agreement that God is answerable to Abraham for what has taken place with the destruction of the Temple in 70 C.E. by the Roman Empire after a Jewish rebellion. God does not impose silence on Abraham, saying that that is a decree not to be contested but only accepted. God as a social being accepts that God must provide sound reasons for God's actions, as must any other reasonable person in a world governed by rules applicable to everyone. Abraham is a fine choice for the protagonist, since he engaged in the argument concerning Sodom. His complaint is expressed at B: God is now called to give an account. At each point, then, Abraham offers arguments in behalf of sinning Israel, and God responds, item by item. The climax has God promising Israel a future worth having. God emerges as both just and merciful, reasonable but sympathetic. The transaction attests to God's conformity to rules of reasoned transactions in a coherent society.

Though in the image of the sage, God towers over other sages, disposes of their lives and determines their destinies.

Portraying God as sage allowed the storytellers to state in a vivid way convictions on the disparity between sages' great intellectual achievements and their this-worldly standing and fate. But God remains within the model of other sages, takes up the rulings, follows the arguments, participates in the sessions that distinguish sages and mark them off from all other people:

Said R. Judah said Rab, "When Moses went up to the height, he found the Holy One, blessed be he, sitting and tying crowns to the letters [of the Torah]."

"He said to him, 'Lord of the universe, why is this necessary?'

"He said to him, 'There is a certain man who is going to come into being at the end of some generations, by the name of Aqiba b. Joseph. He is going to find expositions to attach mounds and mounds of laws to each point [of a crown].'

"He said to him, 'Lord of the universe, show him to me.'

"He said to him, 'Turn around.'

"[Moses] went and took his seat at the end of eight rows, but he could not understand what the people were saying. He felt weak. When discourse came to a certain matter, one of [Aqiba's] disciples said to him, 'My lord, how do you know this?'

"He said to him, 'It is a law revealed by God to Moses at Mount Sinai.'

"Moses' spirits were restored.

"He turned back and returned to the Holy One, blessed be he. He said to him, 'Lord of the universe, now if you have such a man available, how can you give the Torah through me?'

"He said to him, 'Be silent. That is how I have decided matters.'

"He said to him, 'Lord of the universe, you have now shown me his mastery of the Torah. Now show me his reward.'

"He said to him, 'Turn around.'

"He turned around and saw people weighing out his flesh in the butcher-shop.

"He said to him, 'Lord of the universe, such is his mastery of
Torah, and such is his reward?'
"He said to him, 'Be silent. That is how I have decided matters.'"
—Talmud of Babylonia Menahot 29b

When we noticed that we are like God, but we are not confused
with God, this story comes to mind. This is the single most important narrative about the personality of God. Here is the
point at which humanity cannot imitate God but must relate to
God in an attitude of profound humility and obedience. For
God's role in the story finds definition as hero and principal actor. God is no longer the mere interlocutor, nor does God simply answer questions by citing Scripture.

Quite to the contrary, God is always God, never mere humanity. God makes all the decisions and guides the unfolding of
the story. Moses then appears as the straight man. He asks the
questions that permit God to make the stunning replies. Moses,
who is called "our rabbi" and forms the prototype and ideal of
the sage, does not understand. God then tells him to keep silent
and accept God's decree. God does what God likes, with whom
God likes. Perhaps the storyteller had in mind a polemic against
rebellious brilliance, as against dumb subservience. But that
does not seem to me the urgent message, which rather requires
acceptance of God's decrees, whatever they are, when the unde-
serving receive glory, when the accomplished come to nothing.
That God emerges as a fully formed personality—the model for
the sage—hardly requires restatement.

Just as Israel glorifies God, so God responds and celebrates
Israel. Just as there is a "you" to whom humanity prays, so God
too says prayers—to God, and the point of these prayers is that
God should elicit from himself forgiveness for Israel:

Said R. Yohanan in the name of R. Yosé, "How do we know that
the Holy One, blessed be he, says prayers?

"Since it is said, 'Even them will I bring to my holy mountain and make them joyful in my house of prayer' (Isa. 56:7).

"'Their house of prayer' is not stated, but rather, 'my house of prayer.'

"On the basis of that usage we see that the Holy One, blessed be he, says prayers."

What prayers does he say?

Said R. Zutra bar Tobiah said Rab, "'May it be my will that my mercy overcome my anger, and that my mercy prevail over my attributes, so that I may treat my children in accord with the trait of mercy and in their regard go beyond the strict measure of the law.'"

—Talmud of Babylonia Berakhot 7a

Sages' vision of God encompassed God's yearning for Israel, God's eagerness to forgive Israel its sins, God's power to overcome anger in favor of mercy and love:

It has been taught on Tannaite authority:

Said R. Ishmael b. Elisha [who is supposed to have been a priest in Temple times], "One time I went in to offer up incense on the innermost altar, and I saw the crown of the Lord, enthroned on the highest throne, and he said to me, 'Ishmael, my son, bless me.'

"I said to him, 'May it be your will that your mercy overcome your anger, and that your mercy prevail over your attributes, so that you treat your children in accord with the trait of mercy and in their regard go beyond the strict measure of the law.'

"And he nodded his head to me."

And from that story we learn that the blessing of a common person should not be negligible in your view.

—Talmud of Babylonia Berakhot 7a

The consubstantial traits of attitude and feeling—just as humanity feels joy, so does God; just as humanity celebrates God, so does God celebrate Israel—are made explicit. The social transactions of personality are specified as well. Just as Israel declares God to be unique, so God declares Israel to be unique. And just as Israel prays to God, so God says prayers.

What God asks of God is that God transcend God—which is what, in prayer, humanity asks for as well. In the end, therefore, to be "in our image, after our likeness," the power of the powerless, the riches of the disinherited, the valuation and valorization of the will of those who are so humble in this world as to have no right to will, is to be not the mirror image of God but to be very much like God. Then we come to the category that defines the proper relationship of a human being to God: one in which what a person does, does not coerce God but invokes in God an attitude of concern and love for the person.

What, exactly, does it mean to imitate God as God is portrayed by the Torah? Efforts are made at summarizing the whole Torah in a few words. Here, in the famous saying that follows, we deal with a theological generalization in the setting of a fable, no evidence, no argument, no reasoning being included. All we have is simply how a great sage said things should be seen:

> There was another case of a gentile who came before Shammai. He said to him, "Convert me on the stipulation that you teach me the entire Torah while I am standing on one foot." He drove him off with the building cubit that he had in his hand.
>
> He came before Hillel: "Convert me."
>
> He said to him, "'What is hateful to you, to your fellow don't do.' That's the entirety of the Torah; everything else is elaboration. So go, study." —Talmud of Babylonia Shabbat 31a

The framer of this narrative setting for the Golden Rule has given us an allegation, not an argument; we do not know why the ethical principle of reciprocity ("love your neighbor as yourself," Lev. 19:18) takes priority over any of a dozen candidates; we cannot even say how the oral Torah, represented by Hillel's statement, relates to the written one, Lev. 19:18 not being cited at all!

What, exactly, are we expected to be and to do because we wish to be "like God"? The answer is given at Lev. 19:1: "You shall be holy, for I the Lord your God am holy." Our sages of blessed memory spell out the meaning of holiness, and that means, to be merciful and compassionate:

> "This is my God and I will adorn him" (Exod. 15:2)—adorn yourself before him by truly elegant fulfillment of the religious duties, for example: A beautiful tabernacle, a beautiful palm branch, a beautiful ram's horn, beautiful show fringes, a beautiful scroll of the Torah, written in fine ink, with a fine reed, by a skilled penman, wrapped with beautiful silks.
>
> Abba Saul says, "'I will adorn him'—be like him: Just as he is gracious and compassionate, so you be gracious and compassionate."
>
> —Talmud of Babylonia Shabbat 133b

Abba Saul's statement says in a few words the entire knowledge of God that in the end the Torah—meaning Judaism—provides. For all of the truly pious conduct in doing religious duties, the real imitation of God comes about in our capacity to love one another.

To summarize: What we know about God and ourselves we know because God's grace has permitted us that knowledge—that alone. So the proposition is, the facts provided by the Torah themselves comprise an act of grace. This is demonstrated syllogistically, on the basis of three givens, which were listed in the opening sentences. These three fundamental truths govern throughout: humanity is made in the image of God; Israel are children of God; Israel possesses the most precious of gifts. These are givens. Wherein lies the gift? The act of grace is that we are told that they are God's gifts to us. We are not only in God's image—something we cannot have known on our own—but God has told us so. Israel are not only God's children—it would have been arrogance to have supposed so on their own—but God has so stated in so many words. Israel possesses the greatest gift of all. They know it: God has said so. So the syllogism draws on three facts to make one point that is not stated but that lies at the goal of the argument.

> R. Aqiba says, "Precious is the human being, who was created in the image [of God].
>
> "It was an act of still greater love that it was made known to him that he was created in the image [of God], as it is said, 'For in the image of God he made man' (Gen. 9:6).
>
> "Precious are Israelites, who are called children to the Omnipresent.
>
> "It was an act of still greater love that they were called children to the Omnipresent, as it is said, 'You are the children of the Lord your God' (Deut. 14:1).
>
> "Precious are Israelites, to whom was given the precious thing.
>
> "It was an act of still greater love that it was made known to them that to them was given that precious thing with which the world was made, as it is said, 'For I give you a good doctrine. Do not forsake my Torah' (Prov. 4:2)."
>
> —Mishnah-tractate Abot 3:13–14

These six statements form the paradigm of Judaic theology: not truth alone, but truth enhanced because of the Torah's verification and validation. That is what it means to say, Israel knows God through the Torah. God is known because God makes himself known. With that proposition, Islam and Christianity can well concur.

CHAPTER 2

Hinduism

HOW DO WE KNOW ABOUT GOD?

Hindus know about their gods by listening and remembering. The divine, in all of its manifestations, reveals itself through *shruti* (*śrūti*), "what is heard," and *smriti* (*smṛti*), "what is remembered." Let us begin with listening. Hindus believe that knowledge of their gods is contained in sacred sound—sound that has existed eternally, before the creation of the universe, of human beings, of plants and animals. This sound is called *mantra,* sacred speech, and the praise of mantra permeates the earliest Hindu religious compositions, as well as Hindu ritual today. In a poem of one of the very first Hindu texts, the goddess of speech, Vac (*Vāc*), declares:

> I am the Queen, the confluence of wealth, the proficient one who is first among those honored by sacrifice. (Rig Veda 10.125.3)

The earliest version of this way of knowing "through the ear" begins with the four Vedas—oral compositions of people who called themselves Aryans and who were the ancestors of many of the inhabitants of India today. The term *Veda* literally means "knowledge," and these four works comprise the accompaniment to the Vedic sacrifice—the main form of worship for the early Aryans. The first Veda, the Rig Veda (*Ṛg Veda*), is the oldest (c. 1500 B.C.E.), and comprises the mythological hymns of the sacrifice. The second, the Yajur Veda, contains directions on how to conduct the ritual; the third, the Sama Veda (*Sāma Veda*), contains accompanying musical chants. The final Veda, the Atharva Veda, includes hymns for fertility, healing, and other everyday uses in the domestic context, apart from the public sacrifice. All of these Vedas were forms of listening to the gods, since they were chanted meticulously and carefully, and passed down from father to son.

What was this sacrifice—this place of listening to sacred speech—like? In addition to being an arena in which shruti was chanted, sacrifice usually involved an animal or vegetable offering to one of the many Vedic gods. This offering created a link between the world of humans and the world of the gods, and all of the participants within the sacrifice were transformed by such communication between the heavenly and the earthly realms. As a result of this awesome power, the Vedic sacrifice was seen as the mechanism by which the entire cosmos lived and breathed and had its being. Continuing sacrifice not only brought particular gifts to particular sponsors, but it itself was the mechanism by which the truth of the universe, called *rita* (*ṛta*), was maintained. The poet of the Rig Veda praises the gods for dispersing this truth through their light:

> The one who knows your action, that the footless dawn is the pre-cursor of footed beings, and that your child, the sun, sustains the weight of this world: that person spreads the truth (*ṛta*) of light, and disperses the falsehood (*anṛta*) of darkness. (Rig Veda 1.152.3)

This hymn presents the Vedic deities as the divinities that pre-side over days and nights; therefore the dawn and the course of the sun may be considered as their work. The dawn is called *apad,* or footless, not moving by its own feet or steps, but as depending upon the motion of the sun. Thus, *rita* and *anrita* (*anṛta*), truth and untruth, are classed together, not only as beacons of light and darkness, but as the two poles behind the working of the universe itself. In another hymn, the poet proclaims:

> That was the model for the human sages, our fathers, when the primeval sacrifice was born. With the eye that is mind, in thought I see those who were the first to offer this sacrifice. (Rig Veda 10.130)

According to this hymn, the gods themselves performed the first sacrifice—the great mechanism that keeps the world in order and the universe in balance.

Yet there is more to listening to gods than the turbulence and wonder of the Vedic sacrifice. This power of truth, the power behind the sacrifice, was called *brahman*—an important and quite multifaceted word. Over time, shruti, listening to the gods, came to involve meditation upon this all-powerful force of brahman—a practice continued by Hindus today. These thoughts were gathered up in books called the Upanishads (*Upaniṣads*), composed between 900 and 300 B.C.E. The Upanishads consider all facets of brahman—its relationship to the larger world outside the sacrifice, as well as the inner world within the human person. Thus, the sacrificial imagery that is so rampant throughout the Vedic texts becomes internal sacrificial imagery—the fire burning in the body, and the various sacrificial procedures becoming analogues for proper meditation on brahman.

It is important to remember that brahman is not, properly speaking, a god. Unlike the gods, who have personalities and ways of operating all their own, brahman is better thought of as a unifying principle: a principle that animates the entire universe with its power, and yet is as tiny as the smallest fig divided into infinitesimal parts. And thus, one might call this way of thinking not "monotheism," which would mean belief in a single god, but "monism," belief in a single force that enlivens. As the Mundaka Upanishad (*Muṇḍaka Upaniṣad*) 2.1 states,

> As from a well-blazing fire, sparks which look alike fly forth by the thousands, so from the imperishable *brahman*, manifold beings are produced, and go back.

Thus, the Upanishadic answer to how we know god is a slightly different one from the Vedic answer: one should meditate on brahman, in order that one might become liberated from the world of suffering. How did this world of suffering come to be conceived? It was during this time that the notion of *samsara* (*saṃsāra*), or an endless cycle of death and rebirth, came to be central in Indian thought, and it has remained central for Hindus ever since. This endless cycle of transmigration, as it is sometimes called by Western scholars, was activated by the law of *karma*. Briefly put, the law of karma consists in the fact that every action possesses a consequence—either in this life or the next. In addition, every action is based on a form of attachment, which can be either positive or negative; passion for and aversion to a particular thing are equal forms of attachment.

The Upanishadic resolution of this endless round of suffering based on attachment was meditation upon *atman* (*ātman*), the eternally existing "self" of the human person that existed beyond all attachment. Not only was meditation upon atman crucial, but the realization that atman was identical with brahman, that unifying power behind the universe. The Upanishadic sage Yajñavalkya says to his student that he must realize this basic truth: "You are that." "You," or the self, the enduring one that exists beyond all attachment, is the same as "that," or brahman. These ideas about shruti have remained the central tenets of Hindu philosophy and meditational practices for two thousand years, up to the present day.

So much, then, for listening as a way of knowing about god.

What about remembering, or smriti? Hindus know their gods through remembering narratives—stories that are contained in famous epics, particularly two called the Mahabharata (*Mahābhārata*) and the Ramayana (*Rāmāyaṇa*), and in texts called the Puranas (*Purāṇas*), or "stories of the olden times." All of the epics and Puranas consist of mythological exploits of the gods as well as the bardic accounts of individual chiefs, their families and dynasties, how battles were won and cattle raids avoided, how one tribe achieved supremacy over the other. The way the Mahabharata is composed has often been compared to a Chinese box, in which boxes nest within boxes; so too stories are nested with stories. The framing story of the Mahabharata is the warfare of the Bharatas—how two branches of the same family, the Kauravas and the Pandavas (Pāṇḍavas), fight over land and inheritance. Scholars now believe that there are enough archaeological remains in and around Delhi, near where the war is supposed to have been fought, to indicate that an actual war did occur, and several accounts of the war survived. Other stories and plots grew up around this basic "frame tale."

The Ramayana epic, too, contains stories within stories, but its main story is that of Rama (Rāma), a form of the Hindu god Vishnu (Viṣṇu). Rama was created by the gods to kill the demon Ravana (Rāvaṇa), who was plaguing the world. Rama's rescue of his wife, Sita (Sītā), from the clutches of Ravana enabled the balance and harmony in the universe to be restored, and Rama to rule as king in the ancient, sacred city of Ayodhya.

Unlike the epics, tales of the Puranas focus on the ways in which gods make themselves known on earth—through avatars (*avatāras*), or divine forms, come to rescue the earth because it has fallen into a particularly bad state. One Purana tells of how the god Vishnu becomes a tortoise in order to hold the world up in a flood; another tells a delightful story of the household life of the god Shiva (Śiva), and his wife and consort, Parvati (Pārvatī).

All of these stories become part of a Hindu's imagination from childhood; they shape imagination early in life, and become instructive lessons during the temple worship of adulthood. The myths found in smriti are ways of remembering the gods, because they are retold again and again in various contexts of Hindu daily life. Smriti texts are recited in the temples that house the gods. They are also retold in musical household gatherings called *bhajans*, where small groups of people tell the narratives to each other through the night, and the exploits of the gods are reimagined in vivid detail.

One does not remember the gods through narrative alone, however. The smriti texts not only contain stories; they also have a careful system of laws to follow about how and when to worship the gods. These are called Dharma Shastras (*Dharma Śāstras*), and they involve directions on how to follow one's *dharma*, or social role in life. A person's dharma involves commitment to the duties of their particular *varna* (*varṇa*), or station in society. Traditional Hindu society is divided into four parts: the *brahmin*, or priestly, class; the *kshatriya* (*kṣatriya*), or warrior, class; the *vaishya* (*vaiśya*), or agricultural, class; and the *shudra* (*śūdra*), or servant, class. The smriti literature on dharma takes this fourfold classification and designs a way of life for each of these social segments. A priest's dharma is to sacrifice, study the Veda, and perform rites of worship for the gods. A warrior's dharma is to honor the gods by protecting the people. An agriculturalist's dharma is to provide wealth for society, and thereby for the gods who receive human offerings. A servant's dharma is to honor the gods by attending to the needs of the various other classes. Through various examples and accounts of social alliances and daily rituals, this smriti literature illustrates how Hindus come to know the gods through the right relationships between individuals in society.

Finally, Hindus know the gods through devotion, or *bhakti*. *Bhakti* comes from the Sanskrit word *bhuj*, to partake of, or belong to, and a Hindu knows god through "belonging to" a particular god with intense loyalty and fervor. One of the best-known examples of this devotional form of knowing god is in the Bhagavad Gita (*Bhagavad Gītā*), a part of the Mahabharata epic. The scene of the Gita takes place at the very beginning of a great battle between cousins, and the hero Arjuna is faced with the prospect of killing his kinsmen. He begins to tell his doubts to his charioteer, Krishna (Kṛṣṇa). Krishna's advice to Arjuna, and his own self-revelation as the lord of the universe, comprise the eighteen chapters called the Bhavagad Gita, or "Song to the Lord Krishna." While the Gita reached its final form later than the Upanishads, it contains many of their same themes: the role of karma and rebirth, the nature of brahman, and how one acts in order to know brahman.

And yet the entirety of these more philosophical musings are subsumed into worship of Krishna as an avatar of Vishnu. The basic theology of bhakti in the Gita is this: when the law of dharma deteriorates, then the Lord generates himself on earth in an appropriate form. Arjuna, the warrior, is given a vision of Krishna not just as his charioteer, but as the supreme Lord—the Lord of time and space, bright as a thousand suns. Krishna is so immense that he grinds the warriors of the battle into powder with his many mouths. This theophany, or sudden vision of god, teaches that no amount of sacrificial practice, no amount of sheer asceticism for its own sake, no amount of knowledge-seeking alone, is sufficient. As Krishna himself tells Arjuna,

> Set your heart on me alone, and give to me your understanding. You shall live in the truth of me from now on.
>
> But if you are unable to rest your mind in me, then try to reach me through the practice of Yoga concentration.
>
> If you are unable to practice concentration, dedicate all your work to me. By doing action alone in my service, you shall attain perfection.

And even if you are not able to do this, then take refuge in devotion to me and surrender to me the fruit of all your work—with
selfless devotion and humble heart. (Bhagavad Gita 12.8–12)

It is only bhakti, or intense devotion, to Krishna that can provide tranquillity of mind and conviction of purpose. It is only
through giving up all to Krishna that Arjuna can act in the
world.

WHAT DO WE KNOW ABOUT GOD?

Who are these gods that are listened to and remembered? Their
shapes and characteristics certainly change over time. And yet
two things remain constant: Hindus know that god is always
plural—manifest in a thousand different ways, each manifestation to be worshiped as a deity in its own right. Thus, although
it is possible to speak of a single "god" who is important to any
worshiper in Indian religious history, it is impossible to speak
about a single, monotheistic system. The worship of gods in ancient India, and in some sense also today, is best described as a
kind of selective monotheism—the choice of one god over
many possible ones.

Let us begin with early history. An ancient civilization,
called the Indus Valley civilization (3000–1500 B.C.E.), can give
us some clues as to what kinds of gods might have existed in India before the Aryans who composed the Vedas. A large number
of excavated seals give us some tantalizing clues about early
ideas of god. Seals branded with bulls, tigers, and others animals
may have been used as offerings in rituals. One very important
seal, found in the Indus Valley city of Mohenjodaro, depicts a
figure seated like a *yogi,* or ascetic, with his legs crossed, and in
an erect posture. Surrounded by a tiger, an elephant, a water
buffalo, and a deer, he has a horned headdress, appears to have
more than one face, and wears a tiger's skin on his torso and
bracelets on his arms. Probably a symbol of fertility, this image

may also have been the earliest depiction of Shiva, who is also called in later Hindu texts "The Lord of Beasts." From the great number of phallic stones and from the bull's popularity on the seals, we know that this god was worshiped in several different forms by the people of the Indus. Shiva's sign is often that of the phallus, also called the *lingam* (*liṅgam*), which can be seen in the inner sancta of temples today. Here in this Indus Valley seal, then, we are presented with the dual role of a god: he is a fertility deity, and he is at the same time a tamer and destroyer of jungle beasts, the Lord of the Hunt.

Another seal also emphasizes this theme of fertility: it shows a three-horned deity on top of a tree, from whose branches he appears to have emerged. A second figure outside is worshiping the deity in the tree; behind him a bull stands waiting. Around this whole scene stand seven women, who may be dancing around the tree in celebration of a fertility rite. The presence of these fertility goddesses suggests that female symbolism played an important part in Indus Valley civilization. As we shall see in later classical Hinduism, the male god is often depicted as dependent on the female god, a power called *shakti* (*śakti*). What we know about gods from the Indus Valley civilization, then, is that they were concerned with the abundance of the earth and the beasts who lived within it.

While it is still unclear exactly what changed the shape of the Indus Valley civilization, we know that by 1500 B.C.E., an Indo-European people called the Vedic Aryans had become dominant in the region of western India, and were migrating eastward to the Ganges River. The gods of the Vedic Aryans were drastically different from those of the Indus Valley civilization. All of these Vedic Aryan gods, in one way or another, are concerned with the sacrifice—either in providing its power and efficacy or in procuring the actual material of the ritual. Among them, a few emerge as predominant in the pantheon: Indra, Agni, Varuna (Varuṇa), and Soma.

What were these gods like? Indra is, above all, a supporter of
warriors; everything suggests that he was patron of Aryans. "For
success in this battle, where there are prizes to be won, we will
invoke the generous Indra, most manly and brawny, who lis-
tens and gives help in combat, who kills enemies and wins
riches," says the poet of Indra. In contrast, Agni is the fire god
who was also connected with the priests who performed the
sacrifices. He is "fire" under its various forms, but most imme-
diately under the form of the earthly fire that is lit for the morning sacrifice. Poets never tire of describing golden jaws, lock of
flame, seven tongues, and the noise and fright of his burning.
On earth he is intimately connected with human life; he is master of the house and a domestic god, and thus he is ancestral.
Like Agni, Soma has ritualistic and naturalist elements. Although he is only partially anthropomorphized, Soma is the
sacrificial plant made into a beverage, and also made into a god.
Soma gives mystical intoxication, and bestows immortality
upon the sacrificers—immortality best understood here as
"long life." Finally, Varuna is depicted as creator and sustainer
of world: he is the sovereign. He is endowed with the attribute
of *maya* (*māyā*), the faculty of constructing forms. Most impor-
tantly, Varuna establishes and maintains the sacred truth, rita,
in all of its ethical aspects.

All these gods are described in the Vedas, and the descrip-
tions of their actions both in and through the sacrifice make up
a great bulk of shruti; they are the gods that are known through
chanting and listening in the sacrificial arena. Therefore we
must view these early gods not as objects of belief, but as objects
of sacrifice, having identities as receptors of an offering. And as
such, the gods of the Vedas are both beautiful and turbulent.
They are bound up with the natural order, the rising and setting of the sun, the understanding of fire as a mediator between
heaven and earth, and the conquest of enemies through force.

Yet it is not the shruti, but the smriti literature that effects yet another change in what we know about god—a change that is permanent. Both the epics, the Mahabharata and the Ramayana, introduce what is called the "classical Hindu pantheon"—the triad of the gods Shiva, Vishnu, and Brahma. In this emerging new pantheon, Shiva appears as the destroyer, Vishnu as the preserver, and Brahma as the more removed creator god who is frequently associated with the first two. These gods remain the touchstone of Hindu religious practices to this day. There are many theories as to why this sea change took place in Hindu theology; but it is generally agreed that these forms of worship were in place by the fourth century B.C.E., and that the change took place because of two main factors: (1) the rising need for the brahminical classes—the composers of the Vedas and the Upanishads—to address the more popular forms of religiosity going on all around them; and (2) the patronage of kings like the Guptas—who, through their patronage of temple building and the like, put the Hindu god Vishnu on the Indian map in the first few centuries C.E.

Brahma, who is thought by many to be a personification of brahman, the monistic principle of the Upanishads, is a grandfather deity who, once involved in creation, retreats to a place in heaven and only occasionally makes an appearance in the Puranic myths.

Shiva, Vishnu, and the Devi, however, are very different cases. We see the beginning of their theology in the epics. Let us begin with Shiva. In the Ramayana, Shiva calls upon all of the other deities as a congress to stop the work of the evil Ravana from taking over the world. And, he also beckons Arjuna to the mountain in the Mahabharata and trains him in the art of weaponry. While his personality is not fully developed here as it is in the later Puranas, we see the beginnings of his characteristic marks: he is the consummate outsider—the god whose prestige begins and ends because of the fact that he is the outsider. He dwells near the creation ground, his body covered in ashes, his hair in an ascetic's top-knot, and brandishing a necklace of skulls. In one myth, he arrives at a sacrifice given by an ancient sage, and when he is insulted because he is not given the first honor, he creates a conflagration of immense proportions. Shiva is frequently depicted in a yogi's pose: seated cross-legged, alone in the woods. He carries a trident, as his followers do even today, and he possesses a third eye, which can burn his opponents to ashes. His neck is blue, the color of the poison he drank in order to save the gods in their process of creating the world. His symbol is the *lingam*—the male organ, frequently depicted in Hindu iconography as united with the *yoni,* the female organ. In his role of "the destroyer" he is called Nataraja (Naṭarāja), the Lord of the Dance, who destroys illusion. In the more frenzied version of his dance, he breaks the world to pieces at the end of the *yuga,* or cosmic age.

Yet there is another side to Shiva: He is also the erotic lover, the husband who is married to the goddess Parvati, the daughter of the mountain who wins over Shiva's love by performing her own ascetic feats. The myths depict Shiva and Parvati living in domestic bliss along with their children, Ganesha (Gaṇeśa) and Kartikeya (Kārtikeya), in the mountains, accompanied by Nandi the bull, Shiva's faithful vehicle, who can be seen outside almost every Shiva temple in India. This ambivalent nature, of the householder and the ascetic, the outsider who is also an insider, is part of the dynamism of Shiva's worship.

The bhakti tradition of medieval Hinduism, in South India in particular, has taken up Shiva's banner with a vengeance. Most notable are the Shaiva Siddhantas (Śaiva Siddhāntas), "followers of the doctrine of Shiva." These devotees have developed poetry and philosophy about Shiva in both text and worship. He is worshiped as Pashupati (Paśupati), the Lord of Animals, and is bound to souls, who are his cattle. According to Shaiva Siddhanta, the soul needs the grace of god, which according to the bhakti poet Manikka Vachakar is "a love greater than a mother's."

Kashmir Shaivism in the north is another important development of Shaivite worship. Unlike Shaiva Siddhanta, which is more devotional and grace-oriented, Kashmir Shaivism tends to emphasize monism, whereby the soul must realize its true oneness with brahman through knowledge. When Kashmiri Shaivite writers do emphasize devotion to gods, they tend to dwell on the identical relationship between Shiva and brahman; Shiva is not simply the sign of brahman but is the realization of brahman itself.

Also important for the Hinduism of today are the Lingayats (Lingāyats), or Virashaivas (Vīraśaivas), who developed in the twelfth century of the common era. Their practices are particularly noteworthy: they carry the lingam at all times, strung around their neck or held in their hand, and are opposed to images of any kind. They originally rejected the authority of the Vedas and brahmins, opposed sacrifice and even pilgrimage, and gave equality to women. Unlike other Hindus, Lingayats also perform the burial, and not the cremation, of the dead. The Lingayats are quite energetic in their advocacy of Hinduism today.

In contrast to Shiva stands the god Vishnu. His theology is based on the idea of the avatar—the form of god that comes down to earth from age to age in order to address a problem within the world. Even early Vedic texts suggest that the early followers of Vishnu held that god established a set of "entrances" into the world, an idea that foreshadows the avatar theory. They were also known as Bhagavatas (Bhāgavatas), hence the Krishna teaching called the *Bhagavad Gita*. Vishnu's avatars include: a fish to save the world from a flood; a tortoise to churn up the waters of life, a boar that raised up the earth from the primeval waters; a man-lion and a dwarf that outwits the evil intentions of demons. His better-known avatars are the hero Rama of the Ramayana, and Krishna of the Mahabharata and later Puranic texts.

Most of Vishnu's theology is found in the Puranas, beginning most explicitly with the Vishnu Purana (*Viṣṇu Purāṇa*) itself, dating from about the fourth century of the common era.
That Purana, along with the Bhagavata Purana (*Bhāgavata
Purāṇa*), from the ninth century, describes twenty-two avatars
for Vishnu. It is especially famous for its description of the
exploits of Krishna, the best-known avatar of Vishnu. Here,
Krishna's relationship with the *gopi*s, or milkmaids, at his birthplace Vrindaban (Vṛndāban) is developed. This relationship is
called *lila* (*līlā*), or divine play, and includes such exploits as
stealing their clothes, playing the flute, and dancing with each
of them in such a way that each gopi thinks she is dancing with
him alone. As the Bhagavata Purana narrates the scene,

> After multiplying himself so that there were as many forms of him
> as there were *gopi*s, the blessed Lord made love with these *gopi*s—
> even though his delight is in himself, playfully, as a game. (Bhaga-
> vata Purana 7.44.9)

This is the paradigm for the soul's relationship to god. Krishna,
in his divine play, makes himself appear as uniquely adoring of
each individual person who is devoted to him in heart.

One particular lover of Krishna's, Radha (Rādhā), is given
prominence in later bhakti poetry. Radha is the main focus of
the twelfth-century Bengali poet Jayadeva, and of Caitanya, a
Bengali leader of the late fifteenth century. In these poetic
works, and in the explicit theology developed by Caitanya and
his followers, the Gosvamis (*Gosvāmi*s), Radha is seen as the ar-
chetypal devotee of god, a lover who longs for her beloved as
the worshiper should long for god. In this sense, the theology
developed around Radha is based on the model of illicit love,
not married love, because of the emotional tone set by the poetic situation of two lovers separated and yet longing to be
united. Caitanya quite frequently led processions of song and

dance and at times wore female dress to impersonate Radha.
This very strong devotional and theological tradition has led to
a number of famous artistic forms in North India. The *raslila*
(*raslīlā*), in which the life of Krishna is reenacted and the play-
ers are themselves considered avatars of Krishna, is particularly
popular.

Another group from South India, the Alvars (*Āḻvārs*), composed hymns to both Rama and Krishna as avatars of Vishnu.
One particular Tamil saint, Nammalvar (Nammāḻvār), composed poems that were so moving and influential that his works
have come to be called the Tamil Veda and are recited in temples alongside the traditional Sanskritic recitations. Nammalvar's experience is also one of intense devotion, only his work is
particularly infused with protest against the divisions of varna,
or caste. All should be graced by the Lord, regardless of birth or
qualification. As Nammalvar writes:

> Even if they are lower
> than the four castes
> that uphold all clans
> even outcastes to even outcastes
> without a trace of virtue
>
> if they are the servants
> of the servants
> who have mingled in service
> with the Lord
> with the wheel in his right hand
> his body dark as blue sapphire
> they are our masters. (Tiruvaymoli 3.7.9)[1]

Rama, too, becomes a more widespread avatar of Vishnu, so
widespread, in fact, that it is sometimes hard to remember that
he is not a god in his own right. The fifteenth-century poet

Kabir (Kabīr) worshiped Rama, as did the Sikhs; the Sikhs, however, used this name as the more generic term for god, and did not follow the doctrine of avatars. The Hindu poet and playwright Tulsi Das also contributed to the growing theology of Rama by composing the highly influential *Rām Carit Mānas,* "The Holy Lake of the Acts of Rama," in the sixteenth century. This work of Tulsi's is performed in a manner similar to that of the raslila of Krishna: in performing the Epic, actors become avatars of Rama himself. In contemporary India, the Rama tradition has become infused with both devotional and political meaning, as the city of Ayodhya becomes a focal point for the birth of the god Rama. Many Hindus claim that Ayodhya houses a temple that is the birthplace of Rama and that was destroyed by Muslims in the fifteenth century. Thus a great deal of new iconography of and devotion to Rama has developed as a form of Hindu nationalism.

The final member of the classical Hindu pantheon, the goddess, or Devi (Devī), also has a long and complex history. While there is plenty of evidence to support the possibility of a strong mother goddess tradition within the Indus Valley civilization, there are also strong female presences in the Veda: the goddess of speech, Vac, mentioned above, as well as the later forms—Parvati, the wife of Shiva, or Durga (Durgā), the inaccessible one. The main text of the goddess, the Devimahatmya (*Devīmāhātmya*), brings forth and elaborates a theology that is hinted at in earlier Puranas. The Devi is represented as the essence of all three gods, who decide to form her since they are helpless to fight the buffalo demon Mahisa, who is destroying the world. Thus she is the culmination of all divine power. She fights and eventually slays the buffalo demon with her trident, even though he takes on the forms of a buffalo, a lion, and an elephant to thwart her.

Devi is generally represented as having two different forms: first, she may be the terrifying Kali (Kālī) the black—possessing dark skin, tongue protruding, a necklace of skulls, and several weapons. She stands, either naked or with a skirt of human arms, on top of Śhiva; it is said that she gives him her female power, called *shakti* (*śakti*). The most popular theological representation of feminine energy of shakti is that "Without Kali, Śhiva is Shava, or a corpse." The Kashmiri thinker Kṣemarāja gives the following praise to the goddess: "When shakti is known as herself the path, she is the one who makes perfection possible."

Devi's more benevolent form is Gauri, the golden one, and she generally takes the form of the consorts of the various male deities. Lakshmi (Lakṣmī), the consort of Vishnu and the goddess of wealth, and Parvati, the wife of Shiva and mother of their sons Ganesha and Kartikeya, are both manifestations of the Devi in this form. In her benevolent aspect, Devi gives abundance and fertility as the mother. Yet her dark, evil-destroying form is never far from the surface. In this she mirrors the ambivalence of Shiva, constantly moving between the terrifying and the benevolent, the compelling and the repulsive.

HOW DO WE RELATE TO GOD?
THE IMITATION OF GOD

Hindus would answer this question in terms of *puja* (*pūjā*), or honoring god. While the early, sacrificial worldview of Vedic India meant that gods were worshiped in the open air, eventually in the classical period, temple worship developed, in which the god's image was honored in an act called puja. Many of these temples were replicas of mountains, where the gods were said to reside, or of Mount Meru, the mythological mountain depicted in many texts as the center of the earth. In the operations of puja, gods are treated as a kind of royalty, with all of the attendant bathing, dressing, feeding, and cooling that one would bestow upon a royal guest. One manual of worship for Krishna, the *Haribhaktivilāsa,* requires that the temple priest wash Krishna's feet, bathe, dress, perfume, and feed him. Once

Krishna was readied for the day in this way, worshipers would come and perform their own puja, paying honor to the divine guest and making their requests.

Part of puja, and a central part of Hindu theology, involves interaction with the god in terms of both sacred sight and sacred food. Let us begin with sacred sight. When Hindus worship gods, they both behold and are beheld by them. There is a mutuality in the visual interaction, and it is given the name *darshan (darśan)*, literally, "seeing." Because the gods see their worshipers as much as the worshipers see their god, there is a sense of grace, or divine gift, that comes with every sight of god—in the temple, along the roadside, in the kitchen of one's home.

Moreover, Hindus frequently come to the temple with a food offering to the gods. Once it has been blessed and symbolically consumed by the deity, it is returned to the worshiper as *prasad (prasāda),* or the sacred food of the god. Prasad is given out regularly at temples, but is also part of large temple festivals, where part of the joy in attending is that one will be showered with the food of the gods. This too, like darshan, is a kind of divine grace, a gift born of the exchange between worshiper and worshiped. In both of these ways, then, in the symbolism of seeing and eating, there is an interactive process of worship. God is never a static icon in Hinduism, but always a living, responding presence.

Temple worship is not the only way of responding to the gods, however. The practice of meditation is central to understanding the Hindu relationship with the divine. After its initial explanation in the Upanishads, the practice of meditation developed into an elaborate science, called Yoga.

Yoga begins with a theory of knowledge called Samkhya (Sāṁkhya). Samkhya teaches that there are two basic categories of spirit and matter: spirit is eternal and unchanging, while matter, though also eternal, is in perpetual flux. Spirit is called *purusha (puruṣa)*, a word originally meaning "person." This idea of purusha is different from the brahman of the Upanishads: in the Upanishads brahman is a single, unifying principle, whereas in Samkhya there are innumerable purushas, or animating spirits. While, like brahman, purusha is pure spirit and unchangeable, it is unlike brahman in its plurality. Matter, or nature, is called *prakriti* (*prakṛti*). It exists at first in a state of rest, but evolves into different elements under the impulse of purusha.

For Samkhya, the universe is formed from the union of spirit and matter. As male is related to female, purusha and prakriti are also male and female. Prakriti—all matter—is made up of the three *gunas* (*guṇas*), or qualities: *tamas,* or darkness; *rajas,* or passion; and *sattva,* or truth and clarity. All the gunas bind the embodied soul, although sattva, truth and clarity, can help it toward final release from the endless cycle of birth and death by severing worldly ties. Samkhyan philosophers believed in the cyclicality of time, and that the cosmos periodically dissolves and is reformed; this dissolution upsets the equilibrium of the gunas, which reappear in a new cycle. Such a theory of the gunas is present in almost all systems of Indian thought, and very much present in the myths about the gods of the classical Hindu pantheon—Shiva, Vishnu, and the Devi.

Although there was no god in the Samkhya system, it provided the basis for the Yoga system, which influenced a great deal of how Hindus understand and relate to god. Yoga is closely related to Samkhya, but the two are counted as separate schools. The basic text of Yoga is the Yoga Sutra (*Yoga Sūtra*), attributed to the author Patañjali in the second century B.C.E. Yoga differs from Samkhya on two major points. It emphasizes mystical or Yoga practices as means for the attainment of liberation from samsara, whereas Samkhya stresses knowledge more than practice. But more striking is the Yoga's introduction of Ishvara (Īśvara), the Lord, as the object of devotion. Ishvara is a special kind of purusha that is untouched by affliction, karma, fruits, or hopes. Ishvara is omniscient and perfect; he is unlimited by time. He is different in never being affected by nature or karma, as the other purushas are. And he is useful to the soul as a helper toward liberation.

Yoga means "to yoke," in the sense of union as well as being yoked by discipline. Yoga begins to emerge, as mentioned above, in the Upanishads, and thereafter many kinds of religious exercises are called yoga, and many ascetics are often called yogis. The Yoga Sutras of Patañjali (200 B.C.E.) set out eight stages of Yoga: (1) abstention, or self-control; (2) observance, or attention; (3) posture; (4) breath control; (5) sense restraint; (6) mental steadiness; (7) contemplation, also called "first meditation"; and (8) concentration, also called "deep meditation." In the Yoga Sutras, the eight stages are explained more fully, each stage leading to the next in a scientific progression. The idea behind the eight stages is this: *Citta,* or mind, is subject to restlessness. Citta is also subject to the five afflictions: (a) mistaking the noneternal for the eternal; (b) identifying oneself with the instruments of body and mind; (c) attachment to pleasant things; (d) avoidance of unpleasant things; and (e) instinctive love of life and dread of death. When the self is freed from this restless citta, with all of its five afflictions, it can withdraw into its own pure nature. This perfect withdrawal is the state the Hindus called *samadhi* (*samādhi*).

These eight stages are the basic building blocks of Yogic meditation. They form another important Hindu practice for relating to god, and for obtaining release from the cycle of samsara. Together, the eight stages are called the Royal Yoga (Raja Yoga), and they combine a concern for mental discipline with physical posture and control. Hindus use other forms of Yoga as well, to relate to god and to obtain release. Dhyana Yoga (Dhyāna Yoga), or Meditation Yoga, focuses less on breath control than on deep concentration. Mantra Yoga emphasizes the repetition of mantra, or syllables. Laya Yoga, the Yoga of Dissolution, aims at the disappearance or absorption of the self.

Hatha Yoga, the Yoga of Force, is parallel to Royal Yoga, and concentrates on physical exercises, often very acrobatic in nature. Hatha Yoga seeks to attain single-pointedness by discipline, concentration, and fixation upon symbols. In all of these forms of Yoga, god appears as a single symbol upon which the meditator can concentrate. Many Yoga practitioners claim to have supernatural powers; called *siddhis*, or accomplished ones, they claim to be able to be buried alive, become invisible, fly, know their past lives, and know the moment of death. These claims are often sensationalized, and most of the great yogis teach that such magical powers are only a lower stage of development, liable to attachment and falsification. Ultimately, these powers are to be passed over in the search for the advanced stages of Yogic concentration and release.

While the Yogic tradition added the notion of Ishvara, or Lord, to the philosophical system of Samkhya, and combined some of the monism of the Upanishads, the main systematizer of these ideas about meditation remains the great philosopher Shankara (Śaṅkara), who lived around the ninth century of the common era. Shankara's school of thought is called Vedanta (Vedānta), or "end of the Vedas." In his Vedanta Sutras (*Vedānta Sūtras*), Shankara explains how the existence of the self was certain and infinite, and that brahman consisted of existence, knowledge, and bliss. Shankara maintained that the world exists only as the perceived, but not ultimate, reality; it is only maya (*māyā*), or illusion. This doctrine of the absolute reality of brahman has been called "nondualist," or *advaita*. While his philosophy did not involve theism, Shankara himself was a devotee of Shiva, and also wrote poems to Krishna.

Another thinker in this Vedanta school, Ramanuja (Rāmānuja), added a theistic bent. Living in eleventh-century C.E. South India, Ramanuja identified brahman with the god Vishnu, and brought a devotional side to Shankara's more philosophical nondualism. He taught that god is the soul of the body, and souls are not simply māyā, or illusion, since human beings and god exist in a relationship of reciprocal need. Therefore, there is not complete absorption of the self into god, but an eternal relationship within god. Madhva, a third influential Vedanta thinker, went even further than Ramanuja in asserting the theistic nature of brahman/Vishnu, and opposed Shankara's nondualism altogether in a straightforwardly dualistic system. He also taught that some souls will never unite with god, but will always be apart from him. Further deepening his theistic emphasis, Madhva also introduced the god Vayu (Vāyu) as mediator between god and humanity.

Finally, some Hindus use another kind of Yoga, called Tantric Yoga, to relate to god. These Hindu meditators believe in six wheels, called *cakras*, that are best described as concentrations of psychic power. Cakras are placed at different points along the chief vein of the body, which runs upon the spinal column. In the lowest wheel, at the base of the trunk, is the "serpent power," *kundalini (kuṇḍalinī)*, which is normally quiescent but can be awakened by Yoga. Being aroused, the serpent power goes up through the great vein, passing through the six wheels of power and enlivening them, and unites itself with the great center of psychic energy, which is at the top of the vein inside the skull. This center is generally symbolized as a lotus. Awakened serpent power is said to give supernatural knowledge and magical faculties. Complete union of the serpent power with the psychic center in the skull is thought to bring liberation. In many Tantric traditions, the way that this is attained is through meditation on a form of the goddess, called Shri (Śrī). Shri is visualized as the great mother, and detailed knowledge of her allows the kundalini to awaken and union to take place.

RELATING TO GODS TODAY

While puja, darshan, and Yoga remain the principal ways that Hindus relate to god in India today, there has been a shift in emphasis from the medieval period, caused in part by the influence of Muslims and Christians in India. The impact of Islam on the theologies of the Indian gods is hard to measure; on the one hand, Muslim invasions from the north, beginning in the late twelfth century, led to large-scale conversions, particularly in the northwest. On the other hand, individual Muslim rulers, such as Akbar the Great (1542–1605), were famed for their tolerance and even patronage of Hindu practices. Although the Marathas (Marāṭhas) organized militant opposition to Muslim rule in the seventeenth century, on the whole there was a great deal of tolerance of one religion for the other, despite their profound differences. In many areas, taxation was the only way that Hindus were required to pay tribute to the Muslim empire.

The question of theistic beliefs was one of the profound differences between these two traditions. Because the Muslim belief is that no image of a deity is to be made or worshiped, a great deal of destruction of Hindu temples and images within those temples took place during periods of Muslim rule. However, some religious figures emerged during this time who seemed to provide a kind of synthesis of the two extremes: the poet Kabir is an excellent example. Although he rejected caste, the worshiping of images, and many other outward signs of Hindu belief, he remained faithful to the god Rama, and called himself a lover of god's "word." He also called himself the child of both Allah and Rama, and his poetry professes this unity of god. One of his disciples, Guru Nanak, was the founder of Sikhism, a religious movement that began by teaching the essential unity of god as "True Creator" and "True Name." While Sikhism has in fact developed into a religion with its own quite distinct identity, it is important to remember that its historical roots are within this very intriguing time of Hindu–Muslim interaction.

The more accessible period, the colonial period, yields a very different account of the transformation of the ways Hindus relate to god. The Christian West, under British colonialism, influenced the Indian concept of god in some profound ways that have influenced Hindu ways of relating to god today. Socioreligious movements reshaped much of the life of nineteenth-century India, and caused a great deal of inner reform in the Hindu concepts of god. For Hindus of the nineteenth century, idol worship, the power of brahmins, rituals, the limited role of women, polytheism, and the varna system all came under major reform.

Many educated Hindus sought to see progress in terms of a return to ancient texts and righteous teachers—particularly the Vedas and the traditions of passing down knowledge from father to son. They came to see rituals, such as puja and darshan, as extraneous parts of relating to god. Nineteenth-century reformers, like Rammohun Roy, argued for an equivalence between Christianity and Hinduism based on the ethical core of each religion. Both religions were encrusted with superstition and error, he argued, and involved mistaken forms of ritual. Other Hindus of the nineteenth century—such as the saint Ramakrishna and his follower, Vivekananda—insisted that all religions are true, and are to be viewed like the spokes of a wheel. This doctrine justified remaining in the religion of one's birth and made conversion unnecessary. All of these Hindu arguments denied the superiority of Christianity.

The Hindu reform movements advocated a radically simpler way of relating to god than those of earlier centuries: this relationship was built through prayer and scripture, and not through icon and ritual alone. Vivekananda in particular emphasized the philosophical aspects related to god, called the way of knowledge, that the Vedantan philosopher Shankara also emphasized. Vivekananda argued that all reality was a single unity, and that all religious faiths and beliefs could be seen as part of that unity. He made this view quite popular in the West, particularly during his visit to America in 1893. Vivekananda believed that the Hindu way of relating to god was, at some level, filled with possibility, both for India and for the world. Through meditation and study, in the traditional Vedantan way, Hindus could become spiritual leaders in an increasingly fractious and pluralistic international society.

This reform movement also meant the production of Hindu scriptures, analogous to the Bible. Texts like the Bhagavad Gita became available to anyone who was literate, as did the right to speak out on issues through pamphlets, tracts, etc. Thus, during the nineteenth century, Hindus' way of relating to god became more individually based. With the proliferation of translations and emphasis on vernacular languages, truth lay in the text, and it was the duty of Hindus to study these writings in order to find within them a key.

New forms of Hindu religious organization and activism also began to emerge. The British government gave legal recognition to associations with weekly congregational meetings that registered with it, and gave them legal rights to own property. Thus a number of Hindu societies for worship and social service sprang up, all based on the British idea of congregation. Societies purchased properties, built places of worship, schools, homes for aged cows, reading rooms, and hospitals. They bought printing presses, did fund-raising, solicited donations for charity, created financial reports, and invested money. For example, the Ramakrishna Math, a society still thriving today, gave a new form of social service to Hinduism, and Arya Samaj, founded by the reformer Dayananda Sarasvati, brought to Hinduism a system of proselytism with professional missionaries and rituals of conversion. In the nineteenth century, then, the Hindu way of relating to god changed dramatically; the printing press, the presence of Christian mission, and the British government all gave Hindus a more "text"-centered, individualist view of their faith.

CONCLUSIONS

Although Hindu practice today is very different from that of the earliest civilizations of the Indus Valley and Vedic India, there are powerful continuities in Hindus' ways of knowing and relating to their gods. The polytheistic tradition, and the practice of choosing one god among many, has been central to all forms of Indian religious imagination. Hindus still know their gods through listening to shruti and remembering smriti. The gods Vishnu, Shiva, and Devi, and their many local manifestations, still remain the gracious residents of all Hindu houses and temples. They accompany the many practices of Yoga, the search for release from the cycle of death and birth. Devotion to them, in bhakti poetry and song, is a staple of Hindu religious life. The prayer of saint Nammalvar makes the point eloquently:

> Show me your grace
> so that I, your servant
> who loves you without end,
> may reach your feet. (Tiruvaymoli 6.10.2)[2]

CHAPTER 3

Buddhism

HOW DO WE KNOW GOD?

In any discussion about God and the nature of human understandings of God, consideration of Buddhist perspectives can be interesting and instructive, in that it directs us toward a greater appreciation of the tremendous diversity among the world's major religious traditions. If one were to pose to a Buddhist this very question of how we humans know God, as if it were a central concern of his or her religion, one would most likely be met with a response of great bewilderment. This is because the goals of entering into a relationship with God and coming to know God, as the concept is defined by Judaism, Christianity, Islam, and even the monotheistic strains of Hinduism, do not primarily apply to Buddhists. There does not exist for Buddhists a God in the sense of an omnipotent Supreme Being who creates and sustains the universe, watching over humanity in moral judgment, and wielding ultimate control over human destinies and the forces of nature.

Indeed, ancient Indian Buddhist logicians, whose philosophies have directly and indirectly informed the worldview of Buddhists throughout the course of history, went to great lengths to disprove the existence of God as a self-abiding, uncaused First Cause—a position held by many of their theistic Hindu opponents. Basing their arguments on the fundamental Buddhist doctrine of *pratītya-samutpāda*, or "dependent origi-

nation," which holds that phenomena always arise in dependence on other related conditions, the Buddhists maintained
that it is impossible for any cause to exist that is not also an
effect, brought about by something else. For them, God as a
self-abiding, uncaused First Cause was a contradiction in
terms, logically inconsistent and unverifiable.

Furthermore, the idea of God as the final moral arbiter in
the universe has also been problematic for Buddhists. In a fascinating twist on the claims of monotheistic religions, Buddhists
have even gone as far as to say that belief in such a God often
leads to ethical degradation! They have maintained that if
someone thinks that God takes care of all matters, it is easy for
that individual either to regard personal deeds as determined by
fate or predestined, or to believe that God forgives all actions,
right or wrong. In either case, one does not take responsibility
for one's own deeds. Herein lies the problem for Buddhists.
They, like Hindus, subscribe to the law of moral cause and
effect known as *karma* (literally, "action"), which states that the
consequences of one's future destiny are determined by the nature of one's every deed. As it is put in these verses from the Pali
Tripitaka, the canon of the Theravada Buddhists:

> Both the good deeds and evil deeds,
> Which a person performs in this life,
> Are those he can call his own;
> Taking them with him he goes on,
> And they follow after him,
> Like a shadow that never departs.

> Therefore let everyone perform virtuous actions,
> They are a treasury for the future;
> For the merits earned in this very life,
> Are a person's support in the life to come.
>   (Samyutta Nikāya III.1.4)

In short, one's own good actions, past and present, produce the causes for future happiness, while evil deeds lead to future suffering as a result. Any present condition is ephemeral and subject to change, due to the influence of karma and its fruits. Therefore, from the Buddhist perspective, those who place their trust in God are liable to abandon personal responsibility for their actions toward others, and are thereby jeopardizing the eventual fate of themselves and others.

In spite of these critiques of theism, however, most Buddhists are not atheists. On the contrary, a common aspect of the animistic folk religions, which coexist with the institutions of Buddhism in most Asian cultures, is the worship and propitiation, especially by lay people, of a pantheon of spirits or minor deities, male and female, who are believed to exert control over such important everyday matters as health, material prosperity, fertility, and weather. Again, for the many Buddhists who worship these spirits, the concern is not with knowing them or relating to them, but with simply pleasing them, so that the beneficent ones might grant favors and the malicious ones might depart. According to Buddhist cosmology, gods and goddesses may temporarily enjoy greater powers, longer lives, and more blissful pleasures than humans, but they are still subject to the same law of karma that applies to all living beings. Indeed, divine beings may be in an ultimately worse predicament than humans, in that the wonderful nature of their present existence may well delude them into thinking that they are really omnipotent and eternal, and thus no longer need to engage in the kinds of virtuous activities that would continue to earn them a place of privilege in the universe. The likely outcome, then, for gods in these circumstances is an eventual rebirth in one of the lower realms of existence—such as the worlds of the hell beings, hungry ghosts, and animals—where the opportunities for a timely liberation from the conditions of suffering are scarce. The Buddhist scriptures even acknowledge a universal king of the gods, known as Brahma, but they depict him as a kind of divine megalomaniac who, by reason of his superior powers, has wrongly convinced both himself and most humans that he is the creator of all things. This belief is frequently referred to in the Buddha's discourses as one of the most commonly held and mistaken religious views. Furthermore, the stature of the king of the gods is nothing unique to Buddhists. Like Hindus, they believe in rebirth, and hold that all beings have at some point been reborn as this god, due to their karma coming to fruition.

As far as there is for Buddhists a god, in the sense of a being who is deserving of the highest reverence by virtue of unsurpassed spiritual accomplishment, it is surely Siddhartha Gautama, the Indian sage who became known as Shakyamuni (Śākyamuni) Buddha (563–483 B.C.E.). Both the family name Gautama ("Descendant of Gotama") and the epithet Shakyamuni ("Sage of the Shakya Clan") identify him as the son of a chieftain of a tribe of warrior-class families who thrived in the Gangetic plains region of northeast India, just south of the Himalayan foothills. His first name, Siddhartha ("He Whose Aim Is Accomplished"), refers to the prophecy delivered upon his birth that he was destined to become either a universal monarch (a *chakravartin,* a "turner of the wheel of the law") or a Buddha. The title Buddha ("Enlightened One") refers to his ultimate spiritual achievement of becoming "awakened" to the true nature of reality. Other significant epithets, ones that the Buddha used to refer to himself after this attainment of enlightenment, are Sugata, the "Well-Farer," and Tathāgata, "He Who Has Reached What Is So." By virtue of this enlightened awakening, the Buddha succeeded in the goal of completely liberating himself from the bonds of his previous karma and the consequent suffering that it caused. Following his enlightenment, the Buddha spent the remaining forty-five years of his life teaching others the path of intellectual, ethical, and meditative discipline that culminates in the experience of liberating insight, known as *bodhi* ("enlightenment") or *nirvāna* (the "extinguishing" of the greed, hate, and ignorance that cause human suffering).

As far as the Theravada ("Teaching of the Elders")—the Buddhist tradition that traces its origins back to the earliest *Sangha,* or "community," of the Buddha's disciples—is concerned, the Buddha is not a god in whom one places faith as a savior who continues to watch over and control the world. Rather, he is an extraordinary human being who is to be exceedingly honored and respected for his discovery of the way to achieve enlightenment—the ultimate spiritual goal of humanity—and for his gift of compassionately spreading his Dharma, or doctrine, to others, so that this most valuable teaching might be preserved and adopted by people of this historical age. All Buddhists do take a vow to seek refuge in the Buddha, as well as the Dharma and Sangha, but for Theravadins at least, this amounts to placing confidence in the Buddha's exemplary achievements, not in any power of the Buddha to effect their salvation. The Theravadin concept of who the Buddha was is poignantly evoked in the *Sutra on the Great Final Liberation,* a most important source for understanding how Buddhists know the Buddha. As told in this sutra, when the time came for the Buddha to die and pass into nirvana for eternity, the Buddha addressed his disciples with a set of last instructions. He began by telling them:

> Be a lamp unto yourselves. Be refuges unto yourselves. Let the Dharma be your lamp. Let the Dharma be your refuge. A monk becomes his own lamp by continually looking on his body, feelings, perceptions, dispositions, and consciousness in such a manner that he conquers the cravings and aversions of ordinary people. And a monk is always strenuous, self-possessed, and collected in mind. Whoever among my monks does this, either now or when I am dead, if he is eager to learn, will reach the summit.

The message here is straightforward. The Buddha is telling his disciples that salvation is gained by following the Dharma, not by following him. By rigorously applying oneself to the path of ethical and meditative discipline taught and left behind by the Buddha, salvation is possible without the presence and aid of the Buddha himself. Sensing that Ananda (Ānanda), his closest disciple, continued to show distress, fearing that the message would disappear with the teacher, the Buddha further drove home his point by saying:

> You should not think that your teacher's words have ceased and that you no longer have a teacher. Rather you should let the Dharma and the Vinaya (monastic code) that I have set forth be your teacher after I am gone.

Here the Buddha reiterates that he is just a human teacher. By naming no successor save his teachings, he does not even set himself up as the head of a religious order. After soliciting further questions from his disciples, both the Buddha and his disciples expressed confidence in what had been said. As his final words, the Buddha declared:

> All conditioned things are subject to decay. Strive diligently!

The Buddha is saying here that in the face of an unreliable world in which nothing lasts forever, the only recourse is that of self-effort, in which the individual takes personal responsibility for his or her own salvation. Nothing is said about placing any kind of faith in the saving power of the Buddha himself. It may be worthwhile to place confidence in the teachings he has left behind, but only if they are practically applied ("Strive Diligently!") and integrated, not if they are merely accepted on faith. Accepting the image of the Buddha and his teachings as they are presented in scriptures such as this is how the Theravadins—as well as members of other Buddhist traditions such as Zen and Tantra, which place a premium on self-effort in study and meditative practice, and personal responsibility in ethics—come to know the Buddha.

So, in the minds of many Buddhists it is the Buddha's teaching of the Dharma, not any status of his as a kind of god who can save those who place faith in him, that sets him far above the gods as a figure worthy of reverence. Yet another common epithet of the Buddha, "the teacher of gods and humans," tells us where he stands in the cosmic scheme of things. The Buddha and his followers never defer to or receive knowledge from the gods, but vice versa, as the following sutra passage shows. In this discourse, a disciple of the Buddha, by the power of his meditation, pays a visit to the heavens in order to learn from the gods about the reality that transcends all earthly things:

> Then that monk, by entering into the appropriate state of meditative concentration, made it so that the path to the world of Brahma appeared before him. He went to the gods of Brahma's retinue and asked them, "Where do the four great elements cease without remainder?" They said, "We don't know. But here is Brahma, great Brahma, the Conqueror, the Unconquered, the All-Seeing, Omnipotent Lord, the Maker and Creator, the Ruler, Appointer and Orderer, Father of the Past and Future. He is loftier and wiser than we are. He would know the answer to your question." Kevaddha said, "And where, friends, is this great Brahma now?" They replied, "Monk, we do not know how and where Brahma will appear. But when the signs are seen—when a light shines and a radiance glows forth—then Brahma will appear."
>
> Then it was not long before the great Brahma appeared. And the monk went up to him and said, "Friend, where do the four great elements—earth, water, fire, and air—cease without remainder?" The great Brahma replied, "Monk, I am Brahma, great Brahma, the Conqueror, the Unconquered, the All-Seeing, Om-

nipotent Lord, the Maker and Creator, the Ruler, Appointer and Orderer, Father of the Past and Future."

The monk said, "Friend, I did not ask you if you were Brahma, great Brahma. . . . I asked you where the four great elements cease without remainder." And a second time the great Brahma replied as before.

After this was repeated a third time, the great Brahma took that monk by the arm, led him aside and whispered, "Monk, these gods believe there is nothing Brahma does not see, there is nothing he does not know, there is nothing of which he is unaware. That is why I did not speak in front of them. But, monk, I do not know where the four great elements cease without remainder. And therefore, monk, you have acted wrongly, you have acted mistakenly in going beyond the Buddha and going in search of an answer to this question elsewhere. Now, monk, you must go to the Buddha and put this question to him, and whatever answer he gives, accept it."[1]

The monk then quickly returns to the Buddha who, after chidingly likening his disciple to a sailor's bird at sea who returns to his home ship after failing to find land, promptly answers the question about the ultimate reality and how to attain it.

The several references given above to passages from the recorded discourses of the Buddha might lead one to conclude, and correctly so, that one major answer to the question of how Buddhists know about the Buddha and his teachings is through scriptures, particularly those comprising the Sutra and Vinaya sections of the religion's canons, which present the Buddha's philosophical and practical doctrines, as well as the major events of his career. Even the simple epithets that the tradition repeatedly applies to him relate some important things about the Buddha's qualities and roles to those who see or hear them. These epithets also serve as pointers to paradigmatic episodes in the life of the Buddha, which function as sources of imitation and inspiration in the Buddhist world. Such major events as the Buddha's miraculous birth, his sensually indulgent youth, his life-transforming exposure to human suffering, his renunciation of familial and societal life, his six years of experimentation with yoga and asceticism, his discovery of a "Middle Path" (which culminated in his triumph over Mara, the god of desire and death, and in his realization of liberating insight while meditating under the Bodhi Tree), his years of compassionate guidance of others toward freedom from suffering, and finally his own entrance into nirvana at the time of his death, are all intimately familiar to Buddhists throughout Asia.

Even more popular, though, than this final life story are edifying tales known as *Jātakas*, or "Birth Stories," which detail the progression of the Buddha's past lives as a *bodhisattva* (literally, "enlightenment being") or Buddha-to-be. As a bodhisattva, he was often a layperson or sometimes even an animal who always acted out of compassion as he strode the path to supreme Buddhahood. There are hundreds of these Jataka tales, and in the second part of this chapter, which examines the question of what Buddhists know about the Buddha, we will proceed to look at examples of these stories, as well as other key developments that led to the formation of Mahayana (Mahāyāna) ("Greater Vehicle") Buddhism, a tradition that ushered in profound changes in conceptions of what it means to be a Buddha. With the historical advent of the Mahayana, scripture will continue to be a major source for Buddhists to turn to in order to know the Buddha. But in bringing to a close our consideration of how Buddhists know the Buddha, it is most important to note that the religion has always provided other vital means for knowing the Buddha, especially for those many lay Buddhists who cannot read. By listening to sermons delivered by the monks whom they support with alms and robes, by viewing in their temples painted and sculpted murals depicting the great events of the Buddha's past and final lifetimes, and by worshiping at sacred sites where reliquary-shrines (*stūpas*) and offshoots of the Bodhi Tree—potent symbols commemorating the Buddha's enlightenment—are located, illiterate Buddhist layfolk have enabled themselves to know the Buddha in a variety of profound ways.

WHAT DO WE KNOW ABOUT GOD?

Toward the end of the last millennium before the Common Era, there arose new developments in Buddhism that would radically alter what Buddhists to this day, outside of the Theravada world, have come to know about the Buddha. The movements that initiated this change became known as Mahayana ("Greater Vehicle") Buddhism. The followers of the Mahayana considered their brand of Buddhism to be "greater" in the sense of "superior," in that they believed their teachings to be more effectively conducive to the realization of bodhi than those privileged by the Theravada and the other (now defunct) earliest sects, to whom they applied the pejorative collective label Hinayana (Hīnayāna), or "Lesser Vehicle." Mahayanists also regarded their tradition as "greater" in the sense of "more inclusive," in that they perceived it as providing more opportunities for the involvement and salvation of lay Buddhists, who were often seen as being excluded from significant participation in the monastically oriented Hinayana systems. In comparison with the earliest forms of Indian Buddhism, the Mahayana also incorporated a broader range of religious practices—many of which were specifically intended to address the spiritual inclinations of lay people—and was more doctrinally ambitious. Of particular interest for us here was their grander, more deified conception of Buddhahood. In response to the more devotional orientation of its lay followers, as well as to encroaching influences from Hindu, as well as Persian and Greek, religious movements of the time, Mahayana Buddhism came to develop belief in the idea of personalized, universal savior figures in the form of celestial

Buddhas and bodhisattvas of unsurpassing compassion and grace who, in their role of actively intervening in the world in order to help bring all sentient beings to salvation, much more closely resemble monotheistic religions' image of God.

In an interesting way, the decidedly nontheistic early Buddhist sects, including the still flourishing Theravada, in their composition of the widely beloved Jatakas referred to at the end of the first part of this chapter, made a marked contribution to the deification process of the Buddha and bodhisattva figures. Mahayana Buddhists embraced the image of the Buddha as he is presented in these tales. In his many former lives, as a bodhisattva, or Buddha-to-be, he, unlike his final incarnation Shakyamuni, is not primarily directed toward the individual, personal attainment of liberation in nirvana, but is more concerned with seeking the universal enlightenment of all living beings, as well as his own. Toward this end, the bodhisattva of the Jatakas takes on a variety of incarnations, and in each of them he is depicted cultivating certain ideal qualities known as *pāramitās* ("perfections"). For instance, as the leader of a caravan lost in the desert, the bodhisattva saves the lives of his people through the incredibly persistent and strong feat of discovering an underground water source, thus demonstrating the perfection of vigorous salvific activity. In another lifetime, the bodhisattva, as a wandering mendicant, endures the violent abuse of an angry king in order to perfect the virtue of salvific patience. Perhaps the most frequent theme in the Jatakas is the perfection of boundless generosity. On numerous occasions, the bodhisattva gave away all that he had, including his own body, without ever regretting it. One favorite example tells of the bodhisattva as a wise rabbit, who is approached by the god Indra in the disguise of a starving brahmin, or Hindu priest:

> The Bodhisattva was delighted. "Brahmin," he said, "you have done well in coming to me for food. Today I will give alms such as

I have never given before, and you will not have broken the moral precepts by destroying life. Go, my friend, and gather wood, and when you have made a bed of coals, come and tell me. I will sacrifice my life by jumping into the bed of burning coals. As soon as my body is cooked, do eat my flesh. Having done so, you should then take up the duties of a mendicant." Then he addressed the brahmin with a verse:

> This rabbit has no sesame seeds,
> No beans, and no winnowed rice.
> But soon this fire will roast my flesh,
> Then you must eat and dwell in the forest!

When Indra heard this speech, he made a heap of burning coals by his supernormal power, and came and told the Bodhisattva. The rabbit rose from his bed of soft grass and went to the spot. Saying, "If there are any insects in my fur, I must not let them die," he shook himself three times. Then, hurling his whole body into the jaws of generosity, he jumped into the bed of coals, as delighted in his mind as a royal flamingo is when he alights upon a cluster of lotuses. The fire, however, was unable to burn so much as a single hair on the Bodhisattva's body. He felt as if he had entered the Himalayas, far above the clouds!

Then, addressing Indra, he said, "Brahmin, the fire you have made is very cold, and does not burn so much as a single hair on my body. What does this mean?"

"O wise one, I am no brahmin! I am Indra, come to test you!"

"Indra, your efforts are useless. For even if every living being in the world were to test my generosity, they would not find in me the slightest reluctance to give." Thus the Bodhisattva roared.

"Wise rabbit," said Indra, "let your virtue be proclaimed to the end of this eon." Then, seizing a mountain, he squeezed it, and the juice drew the outline of the rabbit in the disk of the moon. Then, in that forest, he placed the Bodhisattva back on his bed of soft grass and, taking leave of him, returned to his own heavenly abode.

The wise rabbit lived happily and harmoniously, kept the moral precepts, and observed days of fasting for the rest of his days, and then passed away according to the fruits of his actions.

When the Buddha had finished this discourse, he expounded the Dharma, and then identified the character in the story:

In that previous existence, I was that wise rabbit.

As if this was not proof enough of his utter generosity, the bodhisattva was called upon once again, the Jatakas tell us, this time in his penultimate life, to exhibit the sort of excellent liberality that can only be born from the development of total compassion for others and the realization of the truths of selflessness and impermanence, all major Buddhist tenets. This story, the Jataka of Prince Vessantara, is the most popular one in the genre, and to many Asian Buddhists it is as well known as the life of Shakyamuni Buddha himself. Over the course of his life, Vessantara succeeds in giving away all of his many possessions. This is not enough, however. When wandering brahmins approach him and ask him for his wife and children, he willingly surrenders them as well. In some versions of this story, it turns out that the brahmins are once again really gods in disguise, who finally return everything to the bodhisattva. As with Job and Abraham in the Bible, he was only being divinely tested. But in most versions he winds up without his family, poor and alone in a hermitage. Interestingly, the layman Vessantara ends up in much the same position as a monk, the ideal Buddhist vocation. For Buddhists, Vessantara is a poignant and impressive example of someone who has taken one of the religion's most commonly advocated lay practices—giving—to its furthest limits. They are not blind to some of the serious ethical difficulties involved in giving up one's family, but in the end they are usually supportive of Vessantara's actions. One Buddhist scripture likens him to someone who rushes an ailing person to a doctor by bull cart. Even though the bulls have to endure considerable pain, the patient is saved. In the tale itself, the Buddha, recalling his own former life, sounds a similar tone: "It is not that he disliked his family, but he loved enlightenment more." By perfecting virtuous qualities like generosity, he could become a Buddha, and by becoming a Buddha, he could help everyone.

Besides the Jatakas, another important development in the first centuries of Buddhism, which strongly influenced Mahayana Buddhism's deification of the Buddha, was the emergence of a splinter group who disagreed profoundly with the Theravadins on a number of key issues. They called themselves the Mahasanghikas (Mahāsanghikas) ("Members of the Great Community"), because when they broke from the Theravadins, they took a majority of followers with them. Of even more interest to us here is the fact that this major sect was also known as the Lokottaravāda ("Supramundane Teaching"), because they attributed transcendental, divine characteristics to the Buddha. According to the Lokottaravadin version of the Buddha's life, known as the Mahavastu (Mahāvastu) ("The Great Affair"), the Buddha, by virtue of his stock of meritorious actions in past lives, had become an omnipotent, omniscient, infinite, and eternal being, who created a magical apparition of himself as the historical Shakyamuni Buddha in order to directly aid the beings in this world in overcoming suffering:

> The conduct of the Blessed One is supramundane; his virtuous roots are supramundane; the walking, standing, sitting and lying down of the Sage are supramundane; the Sage's wearing of robes is supramundane; there is no doubt about this. The Sugata's method of eating food is likewise supramundane. The Buddhas do indeed bathe, but no dirt is seen on them. Their forms resemble gold images; this is in conformity with the world. They make use of med-

icines, yet they are never ill. They use it (medicine) so that the givers will accrue merit. Although able to suppress karma, the Victorious Ones make a display of karma. They conceal their sovereign power; this is in conformity with the world. They manifest old age, although they do not have it. The Victorious Ones are endowed with a host of good qualities; this is in conformity with the world.

The Lokottaravadins also maintained that the Buddha has an unlimited body, which can appear anywhere, and live without sleep, due to constantly abiding in meditation.

What Mahayana Buddhists know about the Buddha reflects the culmination of the historical process just discussed, in which the gloried ideal shifted from the historical human Shakyamuni Buddha to his career as a bodhisattva as described in the Jatakas, and to his divine qualities, first promulgated by the Lokottaravadins. Mahayana Buddhists then extended this same religious revaluation to numerous ahistorical beings believed to have reached the end of, or be far advanced on, the path to enlightenment. Furthermore, there concurrently arose in Mahayana circles the idea that the path of rigorous self-effort and self-reliance, espoused so eloquently in Shakyamuni's final instructions, was too strenuous for the vast majority of ordinary people. Many Mahayana Buddhists have also been deeply influenced by the widespread Buddhist prophecies and similar Indian cosmological theories, which predicted the eventual degeneration of human capabilities to understand and practice the Dharma. Accordingly, in the Mahayana sutras we find a universe populated by multiple Buddha and bodhisattva saviors, who reside in celestial realms commonly known as Buddha Fields or Pure Lands, from where they help to bring to enlightenment, through compassionate grace, all those who mindfully place faith in them. Thus a new type of popular Buddhist religiosity evolved, centered on devotion to and worship

of a large pantheon of savior deities who, by the tremendous
power of vows they have made to transfer their great karmic
merit to the purification of special celestial fields, have created
realms where, unlike our world, conditions are ideal for the
pursuit of enlightenment. Mahayana Buddhists believe that
there are many Buddhas and bodhisattvas who have success-
fully realized their vows, but the Buddha in whom they have
overwhelmingly placed their faith is Amitabha (Amitābha) (in
China: Amita; in Japan: Amida) Buddha, the "Buddha of Infinite Light." Buddhists who subscribe to what is called the
Pure Land form of Mahayana Buddhism desire rebirth in
Amitabha's Western Paradise, known as Sukhavati (Sukhāvatī)
("Land of Bliss"), as the immediate goal of their devotion.
Once rebirth in Sukhavati has been gained, the goal is redi-
rected to the attainment of enlightenment, which is effected
through receiving continuous guidance in the Dharma from
Amitabha and his retinue of bodhisattvas. In the following se-
lection from a Mahayana sutra, titled *The Description of the
Land of Bliss,* Shakyamuni describes this Pure Land to his best
disciple, Shariputra (Śāriputra):

> Then the Blessed One spoke to the Venerable Shariputra:
> "Shariputra, over a hundred thousand billion Buddha Fields to
> the west of here, there is a Buddha Field called the Land of Bliss.
> And there dwells a Tathāgata, a completely enlightened Buddha
> named Amitabha. . . . Now what do you think, Shariputra, why
> do they call that realm the Land of Bliss? Because, Shariputra, in
> that realm beings do not experience suffering, neither with their
> body nor with their mind, and the things causing happiness are
> innumerable. . . .
>   "Shariputra, the Land of Bliss is adorned and enclosed with
> seven railings, seven rows of palm trees and garlands of bells. It is
> beautiful and embellished with four kinds of precious materials:
> gold, silver, lapis lazuli, and crystal. . . . And, Shariputra, there are

lotus pools there made of seven precious materials: gold, silver, lapis lazuli, crystal, red pearls, diamonds, and coral. They are filled with water endowed with eight good qualities . . . and they are strewn with sand of gold. And going down into those lotus pools, from all four sides, are four flights of steps, beautiful and embellished with four precious materials, . . . and all around the lotus pools jewel-trees are growing, beautiful and embellished with seven precious materials. . . . And in those lotus pools, lotuses are growing: various kinds of blue ones, yellow ones, red ones, and white ones, beautiful, splendid, vivid, and as big around as the wheel of a chariot. . . .

"Furthermore, Shariputra, in that Buddha Field, divine musical instruments are always playing, and the ground is pleasant and golden colored. Three times each night and each day, showers of divine mandarava blossoms fall. The beings there, in the time it takes to eat breakfast, can pay homage to a hundred thousand billion Buddhas, by going to other universes. And after showering each Tathāgata with a hundred thousand billion flowers, they return to their own Buddha Field in time for an afternoon nap. . . .

"Furthermore, Shariputra, in that Buddha Field there are geese, snipe, and peacocks. Three times each night and each day, they come and sing together. . . . And when the people hear that sound they become mindful of the Buddha, Dharma, and Sangha. . . . These birds were magically fashioned by the Buddha Amitabha, and their cries are the sound of the Dharma. With such marvelous Buddha Field qualities, Shariputra, is that Land of Bliss arrayed. . . .

"Now what do you think, Shariputra, why is that Tathāgata called Amitabha? The light, Shariputra, of that Tathāgata infinitely shines over all the Buddha Fields. Therefore that Tathāgata is called Amitabha."

Even more active in worldly affairs than the celestial Buddhas are the bodhisattva figures of the Mahayana pantheon.

The most frequently propitiated bodhisattva is Avalokiteshvara ("Lord Who Looks Down"), the embodiment of compassion. Avalokiteshvara is renowned among Buddhists for his ability to take on a multiplicity of forms. The leader of Tibetan Buddhism, the Dalai Lama, is regarded as an incarnation of Avalokiteshvara, and in East Asia, this bodhisattva is worshiped as the female embodiment of mercy known as Kuan-yin (China) or Kannon (Japan), meaning the "Perceiver of Sounds." Like other Buddhas and bodhisattvas, Avalokiteshvara is also known for his *upāya*, or "expedient means," the skill of employing whatever action is necessary to lead beings to salvation. But Avalokiteshvara is especially revered for his immediate responses to faithful petitions for aid in specific situations of worldly suffering. Below he is described in beautiful poetic verse from the *Lotus Sutra*, the single most popular and influential Mahayana text:

> Listen to the actions of Avalokiteshvara,
> how aptly he responds in all quarters.
> His great vow is deep as the ocean;
> eons pass but it remains unfathomable.
> He has attended many thousands and millions of Buddhas,
> setting forth his great pure vow.
> I will describe him in outline for you—
> listen to his name, observe his body,
> bear him in mind, not passing the time vainly,
> for he can wipe out the suffering of existence.
> Suppose someone should conceive a wish to harm you,
> should push you into a great pit of fire.
> Recollect the power of Avalokiteshvara,
> and the pit of fire will change into a pond!
> If you should be cast adrift on the vast ocean,
> menaced by dragons, fish, and various demons,
> recollect the power of Avalokiteshvara,

and the billows and waves cannot drown you!
Suppose you are on the peak of Mount Sumeru,
and someone pushes you off.
Recollect the power of Avalokiteshvara,
and you will hang in the midair like the sun!
Suppose you are pursued by evil men,
who wish to throw you down the diamond mountain.
Recollect the power of Avalokiteshvara,
and they cannot harm a hair of you!
Suppose you are surrounded by evil-hearted bandits,
each brandishing a knife to wound you.
Recollect the power of Avalokiteshvara,
and at once all will be swayed by compassion. . . .
If living beings encounter weariness or peril,
immeasurable suffering pressing them down,
the power of Avalokiteshvara's wonderful wisdom
can save them from the sufferings of the world.
He is endowed with transcendental powers,
and widely practices the expedient means of wisdom.
Throughout the lands in the ten directions,
there is no region where he does not manifest himself.
In many different kinds of bad destinies,
in the realms of the hell beings, hungry ghosts, or animals,
the sufferings of birth, old age, sickness, and death—
all these he bit by bit wipes out.
He of the true gaze, the pure gaze,
the gaze of great and encompassing wisdom,
the gaze of pity, the gaze of compassion—
constantly we implore him, constantly we look up in reverence.
His pure light, free from fault,
is a sun of wisdom dispelling all darknesses.
He can quell the wind and fire of misfortune,
and everywhere bring light to the world.
The precepts from his compassionate body shake us like thunder,

the wonder of his pitying mind is like a great cloud.
He sends down sweet dew, the Dharma rain,
to quench the flames of earthly desires.

Glorification of celestial Buddhas and bodhisattvas has also
led Mahayanists of a more philosophical bent to develop theories about the nature of their manifestations in the universe.
The theory that has most informed Buddhists' knowledge
about these figures is known as the "Three Bodies of the Buddha." According to this theory, Buddhas and bodhisattvas manifest themselves in three different ways. The first is called the
Dharmakaya (Dharmakāya), or "Truth Body." The Dharmakaya Buddha is not a body in the conventional sense of the
word. Rather, the Dharmakaya refers to the ultimate truth of
Mahayana Buddhism, which states that all phenomena in the
universe are "empty" (*shunya*) of inherent existence, and are
thus not worthy of our desirous attachment, which inevitably
causes suffering. Thus, anyone who realizes the liberating insight into the truth of emptiness (*shunyata*) is then able to see
this universal nature of Buddhahood. The second way that
Buddhas appear is by means of the Sambhogakaya (Sam-
bhogakāya), or "Enjoyment Body." Through eons of virtuous
practice, Buddhas and bodhisattvas gain the power to transfer
their karmic merit into these subtle bodies of blissful transformation, which appear only to those who have earned rebirth in
a Pure Land, where these celestial figures reside. Finally, Buddhas can manifest the Nirmanakaya (Nirmānakāya), or "Form
Body." This is the physical body that a Buddha magically takes
on to benefit people in this world. The historical Buddha
Shakyamuni is the primary example of this aspect of Buddhahood.

This theory of the Buddhas' bodies was no mere intellectual
exercise. That it became part of the popular mindset is evi-
denced by the following hymn of praise, discovered among the

inscriptions of Chinese pilgrims at the site of the Buddha's enlightenment in India:

I venerate the incomparable Dharma body of the Buddhas, to be realized by oneself, which is neither one nor many, the basis for the great accomplishment of one's own purpose and that of others, neither being nor nonbeing, like empty space of a single taste, whose inherent nature is hard to comprehend; which is unstained, unchanging, benign, peerless, all-pervading, free from discursive thought.

I venerate the enjoyment body, which is supramundane, inconceivable, the fruit of hundreds of good deeds, powerful, which spreads great brilliance in the midst of the assembly to the delight of the wise, which uninterruptedly proclaims the lofty sound of the good Dharma throughout the Buddha worlds, which is established in the great kingship of the Dharma.

I venerate the magically fashioned form body of the Buddha, which can shine forth anywhere like a fire, in order to "cook" beings to perfection; which, tranquil, repeatedly reveals in different places the Wheel of the Dharma leading to complete enlightenment; which employs many forms and takes away the terror of the three lower realms of existence by the expedient means of taking on various bodies; which, with great purpose, seeks out beings in the ten directions.

With devotion I pay homage to the three bodies of the Buddha, who have as their concern the welfare of all beings, who bring the immeasurable merits of the Mahayana, who eliminate the wrong paths of mind and speech. May the merit that I have accumulated, seed of enlightenment, procure for me the three bodies; may I enjoin the whole world to follow the path to enlightenment.[2]

HOW DO WE RELATE TO GOD?
THE IMITATION OF GOD

As one might well imagine, the various techniques that Buddhists practice in order to relate to the Buddha are largely dependent upon and determined by the diverse ways in which they know the Buddha. In the final section of this chapter, we will examine the disciplines used by practitioners in three different Buddhist traditions, in order to gain a greater understanding of the variety of the religion's approaches to attaining salvation.

Theravada Buddhists take closely to heart Shakyamuni's final instructions to follow the teaching and not the teacher. While the stories of Shakyamuni's previous and final lives are inspirational to them, exact replication of his extraordinary career as a completely enlightened teacher of gods and humans is generally held to be impossible. The individual liberation of nirvana, however, is possible, as long as one fully and continuously applies oneself to what the Buddha called the "Middle Way" leading to the cessation of suffering, which is the core of the Dharma. The Middle Way is moderate in the sense that it avoids excessive involvement in the extremes of sensual indulgence and severe asceticism. Nonetheless it is a stringent discipline, a yoga, designed to overcome the deeply ingrained habits of greed, anger, and delusion which Buddhism sees as the primary causes of suffering. This way, also known as the Noble Eightfold Path, consists of the following practical components:

1. *Right Understanding.* Knowledge of the fundamental Buddhist doctrines about the painful, impermanent, and insubstantial nature of the world, and of the means to attain the blissful, serene state of equipoise known as nirvana.
2. *Right Intention.* Thought that is free from greed, anger, and delusion, and full of detachment and loving-kindness.
3. *Right Speech.* Engaging in truthful, friendly, meaningful, and useful verbal acts.
4. *Right Action.* Adhering to the essential moral precepts of abstention from violence, falsehood, theft, sexual misconduct, and intoxicating substances.

5. *Right Livelihood.* Avoiding professions that harm others such as butchery, soldiering, and all fraudulent or criminal activities.

6. *Right Effort.* Possessing the constancy and courage to eliminate and prevent evil states of mind, which hinder progress, and cultivate and maintain wholesome states of mind, which further progress along the path.

7. *Right Mindfulness.* Fully attentive, nonreactive awareness of everything in one's environment, especially one's own bodily and mental activities.

8. *Right Concentration.* Cultivation of deep, highly refined states of meditative absorption, which are characterized by the absence of obstructive mental states of lust, hatred, sloth, distraction, and doubt, and by the presence of a high degree of tranquillity, equanimity, and one pointedness of mind.

Although these eight components are most representative of the Theravada path, they are all surely principles that every Buddhist holds, to varying degrees. This Noble Eightfold Path can also be understood according to the framework of what are called the "Three Trainings." Parts three to five of the path represent the first training, *shīla,* or "ethical conduct." Morality stands at the base of the religion. The process of transforming one's nature must begin by engaging in compassionate behavior and avoiding harmful behavior, before one can develop further and progress along the path. Lay Buddhists are primarily concerned with this aspect of the path. They place their confidence in the fact that the karmic merit they earn will ensure them future well-being. Eventually, the externalized observance of ethical precepts can be converted into one's inner discipline.

Parts six to eight of the path are concerned with *samādhi* (meditation), the second training. Typically this part of the path is reserved for those involved in monastic training and the full-time pursuit of nirvana. As seen in Shakyamuni Buddha's life, the experience of enlightenment centers on the advancement in meditation. The cultivation of deep states of meditative absorption is particularly important in the process of developing detachment from the sensory world of desire. The great degrees of serenity, even-mindedness, concentration, and awareness produced by meditation practice are seen by most Buddhist traditions as absolutely necessary prerequisites to the attainment of the third and final training. This is *prajna* (*prajñā*), or "insight." It is insight into the true nature of reality that finally destroys the ignorance and craving that cause suffering. For Theravada Buddhists, it is the realization that the world is truly characterized by suffering, impermanence, and insubstantiality that will finally eliminate desirous attachment and ignorance, thus producing the liberated state of nirvana.

While the practice of the Theravada predominates in the South Asian and Southeast Asian countries of Sri Lanka, Myanmar (Burma), Thailand, Laos, and Cambodia, the prevailing form of practice in China and Japan has long been the Pure Land school of Mahayana Buddhism. It is true that other forms of the Mahayana, such as the Meditation school (most commonly known in the West by its Japanese name, Zen), with its demanding program of rigorous contemplation, have also enjoyed wide appeal in East Asia, including the countries of Korea and Vietnam. However, it is this highly devotional Pure Land school, with its advocation of simple faith in the saving grace of divine Buddhas and bodhisattvas who reside in heavenly paradises, that has most captured the religious imagination of East Asian Buddhists. Imbued with the sense that we continue to live in an age of degenerate Dharma, Pure Land Buddhists maintain that at present their practice remains the only genuinely efficacious one. Over the course of history, Pure Land Buddhists have engaged in a variety of devotional activities, ranging from ritual worship of sacred images, to public good works and complex visualization exercises, in order to appeal to a Buddha and thus assure themselves of a rebirth in a Buddha Field. One single practice, however, has emerged over time as the mainstay of Pure Land tradition. Called the *nembutsu* in Japan (Chinese: *nian-fo*), this is the mindful recitation of a Buddha's name. For example, Japanese devotees of Amida Buddha have faith that this Buddha will respond to their sincere recitation of the formula, *"Namu Amida Butsu"* ("I Praise Amitabha Buddha"). In the following selection from a Chinese ritual text composed in the early eleventh century by the Pure Land master Shandao, instructions are provided for the practitioner who is seeking to make good on Amitabha's vow that anyone who repeats his name ten times will gain rebirth in his Land of Bliss:

> Every morning, when the sky begins to lighten, having dressed and finished your ablutions, turn to face the west. Stand perfectly erect with palms joined in reverence and, in a continuous vocal stream, intone the name of Amitabha Buddha (*"A-mi-tuo-fuo"*). The time it takes to exhaust one breath constitutes one moment of recollection. Hence, ten breaths are what we call "ten moments of mindfulness." You should chant in accordance with the length of the breath, and not set any specific limit on the number of Buddha recitations. . . . Proceeding in this way, one should string together ten breaths, without there being any interruption. Your attention should be focused on preventing the mind from wandering, for pure concentration is what brings success. . . .
>
> After you have performed mindful recitation, make the following vow and dedications of merit:
>
> "I, disciple so-and-so, with all my heart entrust my life to Buddha Amitabha of the Land of Bliss. May he illumine me with his pure radiant light and enfold me in his loving vow. I have just completed ten moments of mindful recitation of the Tathāgata's name, all done with perfect concentration. In the quest for supreme enlightenment, I seek rebirth in a Pure Land. . . .

"I now resolve myself that, from this moment forward, I will not commit the five heinous crimes or slander the Mahayana. I pray that these ten moments of mindfulness may enter into the ocean of the Tathāgata's great vow. And I pray that, through receiving the Buddha's loving grace, my sins may be eliminated and the foundational cause for my rebirth in the Pure Land strengthened.

"When the end of my life approaches, may I be aware that the moment has arrived. May my body be free of illness and suffering, and may my heart be without attachment or regret. May my mind be free of confusion and distraction, as though I were entered into meditative absorption itself. May the Buddha and his retinue, bringing in their hands the golden pedestal, come to greet me and, in a flash of light, lead to rebirth in the Land of Bliss. . . . May I see the Buddha Amitabha instantly manifest the wisdom, save all beings on a vast scale, and fulfill the vow of enlightenment."[3]

The Tantric tradition known as the Vajrayana (Vajrayāna) ("Thunderbolt Vehicle") is practiced by Buddhists in the greater Tibetan cultural area, as well as by Buddhists in the Himalayan kingdoms of Sikkim, Nepal, and Bhutan. The main practice of Tantric Buddhism, known as Deity Yoga, is a fascinating synthesis of Mahayana devotionalism and sophisticated meditative disciplines. Tantric Buddhists believe that within the human body there reside dormant but extremely forceful divine energies which, if properly awakened through special esoteric techniques, have the power to rapidly transform a person into a completely enlightened Buddha. In Tantra, one's "real" gross physical organs play a secondary role to certain subtle energy centers and channels, in which powerful spiritual forces, in the subtle forms of winds and liquid drops, can be awakened. The Tantric path to salvation is thus effectively facilitated by techniques designed to awaken these untapped forces, which can transform a human being into a divine, liberated being.

What is unique about Deity Yoga is that the practitioner attempts to expeditiously actualize the various bodies of a Buddha or bodhisattva by engaging in an imaginative ritual imitation of a chosen divine figure. Deity Yoga involves simultaneous performance of three major components. The first is meditative visualization of the deity. This practice enables one to replicate and actualize the mental qualities of the deity. The second aspect is the enactment of specified hand gestures known as *mudras* (*mudrās*). Displaying such physical movements allows one to appropriate the body of the deity. The third is repetition of sacred verbal formulas called *mantras*. Mantras are thought to have magical power, and through their repetition one identifies with the vocal acts of the deity. Thus the mastery of Deity Yoga practice results in the complete realization—mind, body, and speech—of Buddhahood. It could be said that Tantric Buddhists relate to the Buddha by discovering the Buddha that lies within.

The following passage is a selection from an eleventh-century anthology of Tantric ritual practices titled *A Garland of Realizations*. It describes a session of Deity Yoga dedicated to the deity Tara ("Savioress"). Tara enjoys a special place in the Vajrayana pantheon because she combines the incomparable compassion of a bodhisattva like Avalokiteshvara and the perfected insight of a Buddha like Amitabha:

> Thereupon, one should bring to mind [a] detailed [visual image of] blessed holy Tara. [One should see her as] proceeding from the yellow germ-syllable *Tam* resting on the spotless orb of the moon within the filaments of the full blown blue lotus in the middle of the lunar orb, originally visualized in one's own heart. One should conceive her to be of a deep green color, with two arms, with a smiling face, endowed with all the most incomparable virtues, and free of every defect, without exception. She is adorned with ornaments of heavenly precious substances such as gold, rubies,

and pearls, her two breasts decorated with hundreds of lovely gar-
lands and necklaces, her two arms wrapped in heavenly bracelets
and bangles, her hips adorned with the beautiful splendor of the
glittering rows of flawless gems on her girdles, her two feet beau-
tified by golden anklets set with multi-colored gems, her lovely
matted hair entwined with fragrant wreaths of flowers like those
of paradise. In her resplendent jeweled headdress is the blessed
Amoghasiddhi, the Tathāgata. She is a shapely corporeal image, a
radiant and most seductive semblance, in the prime of her youth,
her eyes [the color] of a spotless blue lotus blossom in autumn, her
body dressed in all [sorts] of heavenly fabrics and garments, seated
in the half-lotus posture, within a circle of white rays on a white
lotus as large as a cartwheel. With her right hand she is granting all
boons. In her left hand she holds a lotus in full bloom. . . .

After worshipping her in this manner, again and again, and
praising her, one exhibits the hand gesture [appropriate to the vi-
sualization]. First one cups the hands. Then, one extends the two
middle fingers to form a wedge. Bending slightly the three joints
of the first two fingers, one keeps the two index fingers [as they
were]. Holding the thumbs parallel to each other, one holds their
three joints close together. Extending the two ring-fingers to form
a hollow, one joins and extends out the little fingers. This is called
the "open blue lotus" hand gesture.

After one has propitiated with this hand gesture the Blessed
One in her aspect as the essence of knowledge, one should cultivate the incantation appropriate to her aspect as the essence of
compassion. In this manner one should strengthen the conviction
that these two aspects are non-dual. . . .

Also, for as long as one does not feel tired, one may continue
to develop [these visualizations]. . . .

When one feels tired from developing [these visualizations],
one may rest by uttering the incantation: *Om tare tuttare ture
svaha*. . . . For, it is said that this incantation of Tara is truly powerful, and that even all the Tathāgatas salute, worship, and honor it.

Emerging from trance, the yogi sees the whole universe in the form of Tara, and moves about freely, seeing himself as the blessed Tara.

At the very least, the eight great magical powers fall at the feet of one who cultivates [the visual image] of the Blessed One following the process above. What need is there to speak of other powers, which come to him as a matter of course? Whoever goes to a secluded mountain cave and cultivates [the visual image] of the Blessed One, will behold her with his own eyes. And the Blessed One herself will give this person her in-breath and out-breath. Why say more? In the very palm of the hand of such a person she will place even the state of Buddhahood, so hard to attain.[4]

CHAPTER 4

Islam

HOW DO WE KNOW ABOUT GOD?

Muslims know about God both directly, through personal experience, and indirectly through the experience of others. Muslims believe that God is the creator and sustainer of the universe, so signs of his glory can be found everywhere in the natural world—a person can know God merely by smelling a rose and remembering where that rose came from. Another direct way of perceiving God is through the prophets and scriptures he has sent into the world, including the Qur'ān, God's own speech. Muslim mystics also believe that if they follow a path of practice, they will be led to unity with God. While these direct methods of knowing God are available to every Muslim, God can also be apprehended indirectly through histories and legends.

The Qur'ān, God's revelation to the prophet Muḥammad (d. 632 C.E.), urges Muslims to look for God in nature.

Blessed be He in whose hand is the Kingdom—He is powerful over everything—

who created death and life, that He might try you which of you is fairest in works; and He is the All-mighty, the All-forgiving—

who created seven heavens one upon another. Thou seest not in the creation of the All-merciful any imperfection. Return thy gaze; seest thou any fissure?

Then return thy gaze again, and again, and thy gaze comes back to thee dazzled, aweary. (The Kingdom, 67:1–4)

Another verse from the same sura makes a similar point:

Have they not regarded the birds above them spreading their wings, and closing them? Naught holds them but the All-merciful. Surely He sees everything. (The Kingdom, 67:19)

The Sura of the Kingdom was revealed to Muḥammad while he was preaching in the Arabian trading town of Mecca around the year 620. Surrounded by vast reaches of rocky desert and tall, craggy mountains, the Meccan people were well aware of the magnificence of nature. The Qur'ān calls on these Meccans to take the natural world as a testimony of God's majesty and awesome power. Whereas the works of humankind —buildings, clothes, pottery—may have mistakes and imperfections, God's creation is complete.

At times, the Qur'ān is downright angry at the forgetfulness of humankind, at its arrogance in not remembering God's grace every day. The Arabian Peninsula, after all, was a dangerous place in which humankind was almost insignificant compared to vast mountains and trackless wastelands. On the other hand, this bleak land could also be beautiful; a single rainfall could cause the desert to come to life with grasses and flowers. Meccans knew their environment intimately, but ascribed life and death to fate. The Qur'ān urged them to "remember" that God was the source of life.

Perish Man! How unthankful he is!
Of what did He create him?
Of a sperm-drop
He created him, and determined him,
then the way eased for him,

then makes him to die, and buries him,
then, when He wills, He raises him.
No indeed! Man has not accomplished His bidding.

Let Man consider his nourishment.
We poured out the rains abundantly,
then We split the earth in fissures
and therein made the gains to grow
and vines, and reeds,
and olives, and palms,
and dense-tree'd gardens,
and fruits, and pastures,
an enjoyment for you and your flocks.

(He Frowned, 80:16–32)

These verses were revealed at the beginning of Muḥammad's mission to the Meccans, around 617. Indeed, the difference in tenor is readily apparent, as the Qur'ān makes its point in short verses that employ imagery and metaphor. Short verses are the hallmark of early revelation, while long verses are common in later suras. Here, not only is God responsible for the grand works of creation, death and resurrection, but God is also the source of every good plant and garden. Moreover, the Qur'ān emphasizes that this creation has been made for a specific purpose: the "enjoyment" of humankind and God's other creatures.

Suras from the Medinan period of revelation, stretching from Muḥammad's flight (the hijrah) from Mecca to Medina in 622 to his death in 632, are markedly different from Meccan suras. The hijrah marked the establishment of a new community of Muslims and is year one in the Muslim calendar, just as Christians mark their first year with the birth of Jesus. The Medinan verses of the Qur'ān still identify nature as a sign of God, but also urge Muslims to know God through obedience to divine law.

And the beasts of sacrifice—We have appointed them for you as among God's waymarks; therein is good for you. So mention God's Name over them, standing in ranks; then, when their flanks collapse, eat of them and feed the beggar and the suppliant. So We have subjected them to you; haply you will be thankful. (The Pilgrimage, 22:37)

This single verse from a Medinan sura is as long as several Meccan verses combined. As above, nature is created to serve as "enjoyment" of humankind, and the slaughtered animal is called a waymark of God, a sign along the road that God has laid out for his creatures to follow. In this particular case, Muslims are called to demonstrate their remembrance of God's goodness by invoking God's name before killing and eating animals. The proper words for this invocation are: "In the name of God, the Merciful, the Compassionate" (*bismillāhi r-raḥmāni r-raḥīm*). This invocation is found at the beginning of almost every sura of the Qur'ān, above doors to houses, and on the bumpers of cars. Pious Muslims say this phrase before undertaking any task of importance.

In the above citations from the Qur'ān, God is seen as being intimately involved with his creation, not only at the beginning of time, but at every moment. This description of God's creative activity led many Muslim theologians to adopt an atomistic view of the world, that is, a world in which every atom of each tree, rock, and creature was being held in place—indeed was being constantly re-created—by God in every moment. God's power in this system is almost overwhelming. Not only does he determine the position of all the atoms everywhere in the universe at every given moment, but he also determines their individual characteristics and the characteristics of the bodies they comprise. With God holding every atom in place, the fact that "Thou seest not in the creation of the All-merciful any imperfection" is truly cause for a person to "return thy gaze again, and again, and thy gaze comes back to thee dazzled, aweary." Finally, since God created everything, each atom of existence and each person is by nature *muslim,* or submissive to God's will. So confessing the religion of Islam, from the Muslim viewpoint, is merely accepting one's true nature.

Modern Muslim authors also turn to nature as a fundamental way for humankind to know God. Fazlur Rahman (d. 1988) was professor of Islamic thought at the University of Chicago for many years and the author of several books on Islamic theology and philosophy. In a discussion of the role of nature in Islam, he wrote:

> This gigantic machine, the universe, with all its causal processes, is the prime "sign" (*āya*) or proof of its Maker. Who else but an infinitely powerful, merciful, and purposeful Being could have brought in existence something with dimensions so vast and an order and design so complex and minute?[1]

For Rahman, the scientific discoveries of the past century do not undermine the role God has in creation; rather, they reinforce it. As physicists and biologists delve deeper into the mysteries of nature, they are only uncovering the intricate detail of God's flawless handiwork. Yes, Rahman is saying, atoms are made of gluons, protons, and neutrons, but who put them together in the first place?

God's creation of the universe is a sign for anyone to see, but it only addresses one side of human nature. God also appeals to human emotion and intellect through prophets and revelation, and through these media, Muslims come to know God. Although Muḥammad is seen as the last prophet and the Qur'ān as the most perfect revelation, Muslims believe that God has sent many prophets into the world. The major prophets of Judaism are all mentioned in the Qur'ān, as well as Jesus (who is considered by Muslims to be a prophet, not the son of God) and other Arab prophets. Throughout history, Muslims have accepted adherents of other religions (such as Zoroastrians) as recipients of revelation, and to this day many Muslim countries have substantial non-Muslim populations. Among the many familiar stories in the Qur'ān is this version of the Noah story:

> And it was revealed to Noah, saying, "None of thy people shall believe but he who has already believed; so be thou not distressed by that they may be doing.
>
> "Make thou the Ark under Our eyes, and as We reveal; and address Me not concerning those who have done evil; they shall be drowned."
>
> So he was making the Ark; and whenever a council of his people passed by him they scoffed at him. He said, "If you scoff at us, we shall surely scoff at you, as you scoff, and you shall know to whom will come a chastisement degrading him, and upon whom there shall alight a lasting chastisement."
>
> Until, when Our command came, and the Oven boiled, We said, "Embark in it two of every kind, and thy family—except for him against whom the word has already been spoken—and whosoever believes." And there believed not with him except a few.
>
> He said, "Embark in it! In God's Name shall be its course and its berthing. Surely my Lord is All-forgiving, All-compassionate."
>
> So it ran with them amid waves like mountains; and Noah called to his son, who was standing apart, "Embark with us, my son, and be thou not with the unbelievers!"
>
> He said, "I will take refuge in a mountain, that shall defend me from the water." Said he, "Today there is no defender from God's command but for him on whom He has mercy." And the waves came between them, and he was among the drowned. (Hood, 11:38–45)

Like Muḥammad, Noah received prophetic knowledge from God when God spoke to him, telling him to build the ark in preparation for the great flood. Nature, of course, is entirely under God's control, and humankind can do nothing against it without God's help.

The fact that this story is also found in the written Torah (Genesis, chapter 7) does not take away from the importance of the Qur'ān, for all revelation is understood as a proper source for divine knowledge. In fact, the Qur'ān itself is only the most perfect reflection of God's original "Book" for humankind, which is in a guarded tablet with God. Therefore, "the Book" is another term for the Qur'ān, which was revealed in Arabic, the language of the Arabs, just as other scriptures are revealed in appropriate languages for their peoples.

> God there is no god but He, the Living, the Everlasting.
> He has sent down upon thee the Book with the truth, confirming what was before it, and He sent down the Torah and the Gospel aforetime, as guidance to the people, and He sent down the Salvation. (The House of Imran, 3:1–2)

So believers are to turn to the scriptures to learn about God, since it is a "guidance to the people." God has sent guidance many times, throughout history, but people constantly forget, turn insolent, and begin to worship idols. The Qur'ān often speaks of the importance of these prophets and their relationship with an unbelieving people.

> Those are they to whom We gave the Book, the Judgment, the Prophethood; so if these disbelieve in it, We have already entrusted it to a people who do not disbelieve in it.
> Those are they whom God has guided; so follow their guidance. Say: "I ask of you no wage for it; it is but a reminder unto all beings."
> They measured not God with His true measure when they said, "God has not sent down aught on any mortal." Say: "Who sent down the Book that Moses brought as a light and a guidance

to men? You put it into parchments, revealing them, and hiding much; and you were taught that you knew not, you and your fathers." (Cattle, 6:89–91)

In this passage, it is clear that not every scripture is as perfect a reflection of the "guarded tablet" as the Qur'ān. In fact, the Torah and the Gospel are understood to have been corrupted over time by people who wished to lead the believers astray; the Torah was put "into parchments," which revealed some portions but hid others. The fact that the Qur'ān is God's perfect message—God's very speech—has led Muslims to venerate it. In fact, Muslims believe that when reading the Qur'ān, they are communing with God.

Al-Ghazzālī (d. 1111), an important Muslim theologian who effected a resolution between orthodox Islam and mysticism in his great work *The Revivication of the Religious Sciences*, conceived of the Qur'ān as God's speech "concealed in the garment of letters."[2] The idea of reading God's own speech is so overwhelming to some Muslims that they lose consciousness. Al-Ghazzālī tells the story of one of the Prophet's companions, 'Ikrima b. Abī Jahal (d. 636), who, "when he opened the scriptures for reading, would nearly fall faint saying, 'This is the speech of my Lord, this is the speech of my Lord!'"[3] Muslims believe that the Qur'ān ought to be read aloud (the word *qur'ān* actually means "recitation") and in Arabic. Even those Muslims whose native tongue is not Arabic learn to recite the Qur'ān in the language in which it was revealed in order to have the experience of reading God's own speech. Al-Ghazzālī describes the three grades of Qur'ān recitation, from lowest to highest, demonstrating the different ways Muslims experience God while reading the Qur'ān.

There are three grades of Qur'ān recitation. The lowest grade is when the worshipper supposes that he or she is reciting the

Qur'ān to God, standing in front of Him, and [God] is looking at [the reciter] and listening. In this case, one's mental condition is that of begging, praising and entreating [God] and making supplication to Him.

The second grade is when one witnesses with one's heart that God is seeing [the reciter], proclaiming His benevolence, and secretly conferring on [the reciter] His gifts and beneficence. So [the reciter's] station is one of modesty, magnification, attentiveness and understanding.

The third grade is when one is seeing the speaker in the speech and His attributes in the words. One does not think of oneself nor the recitation, nor the relation of divine gifts to the reciter, inasmuch as he or she would receive them; rather [the reciter] confines his or her care to the speaker, and concentrates all thought on Him as if engrossed in the vision of the speaker, apart from anything else.[4]

Al-Ghazzālī's gradations reveal his mystical inclinations, since the highest grade is close to mystical union with the divine presence. But even in the lowest grade, the reciter imagines that she is speaking directly to God, while in the second grade, God is speaking from the words of the Qur'ān to the reciter. Thus, Qur'ān recitation is a conversation with God in which God reveals his benevolence and confers gifts on the reciter.

The third way to know God is through direct mystical experience of union with God. If in creation God appeals to the believer through senses, and in the Qur'ān through reason and emotion, in mysticism God appeals to the believer through the heart. The ultimate goal of the mystic is knowledge of God, and the way to achieve this goal is called the mystical path. The Muslim mystics are known as Sufis, and they have been a part of the Islamic tradition from the first century. Beginning as an ascetic movement in reaction against the opulent lifestyle of some early Muslim leaders, Sufism eventually developed its own unique interpretations of Islamic tradition. It would be wrong, however, to characterize Sufism as a later, non-Islamic movement, since many Qur'ānic passages use metaphoric language, which lends itself easily to a mystical reading. Perhaps the most famous of these verses is that of the Sura of Light.

> God is the Light of the heavens and the earth; the likeness of His Light is as a niche wherein is a lamp (the lamp in a glass, the glass as it were a glittering star) kindled from a Blessed Tree, an olive that is neither of the East nor of the West whose oil wellnigh would shine, even if no fire touched it; Light upon Light; (God guides to His Light whom He will.) (And God strikes similitudes for men, and God has knowledge of everything.)
>
> in temples God has allowed to be raised up, and His Name to be commemorated therein; therein glorifying Him, in the mornings and the evenings,
>
> are men whom neither commerce nor trafficking diverts from the remembrance of God and to perform the prayer, and to pay the alms, fearing a day when hearts and eyes shall be turned about,
>
> that God may recompense them for their fairest works and give them increase of His bounty; and God provides whomsoever He will, without reckoning.
>
> And as for the unbelievers, their works are as a mirage in a spacious plain which the man athirst supposes to be water, till, when he comes to it, he finds it is nothing; there indeed he finds God, and He pays him his account in full; (and God is swift at the reckoning.)
>
> or they are as shadows upon a sea obscure covered by a billow above which is a billow above which are clouds, shadows piled one upon another; when he puts forth his hand, wellnigh he cannot see it. And to whomsoever God assigns no light, no light has he. (Light, 24:35–40)

Without knowing anything about Sufism, it is easy to see that these verses lend themselves to a representation of Islam as a mystery. God is light and spreads his light through the world. Those who see this light remember God and his mercy through performance of the duties of prayer and almsgiving. But not everyone can perceive this light, this mystery, since many are covered with billows and clouds so thick that they cannot even see their own hands in front of them.

Individual Sufis interpreted the metaphors in different ways. Ibn al-'Arabī (d. 1240), the Spanish mystic who developed a grand system of theosophy, understood the oil to refer to the human being before the fire (God's spirit) touches it. According to Ibn al-'Arabī, the human potential for right action is so great that it can almost achieve good works on its own; this is the meaning of the statement that the "oil wellnigh would shine, even if no fire touched it." God's goodness in proximity of this potential is the meaning of the phrase "Light upon Light." Other interpreters have seen God's light as Muḥammad, the niche as Muḥammad's breast, and the lamp as the light of knowledge, or prophecy. Finally, al-Ghazzālī explains the meaning of the billows, describing the first as lust, the second as ferocious attributes, such as wrath, enmity, and hatred, and the cloud as wrong belief and heresy. The implication is that those who do not believe are prevented from seeing the light by their own evil urges.

From al-Ghazzālī's interpretation, it is clear that Sufis understand that one can gain knowledge of God through purification, ridding oneself of "clouds" such as lust and hatred, which hide the light of God. The precise nature of the mystical path varied with time and place, but it often included vows of poverty and a commitment to follow a spiritual guide. A special form of prayer, known as the *dhikr*, was prescribed, involving repetition of a phrase or word. Dhikr means both "remembrance" and "repetition." So while the mystic adepts were repeating the name of God (Allāh) or the statement "there is no god but God" (*lā ilāha illā-llāh*), they were also remembering God's goodness and mercy, according to the Qur'ānic command. These practices were to lead to a mystical experience of union with God through denial of all other sensory information. Consider again al-Ghazzālī's description of the third stage of Qur'ān recitation:

> The third grade is when one is seeing the speaker in the speech and His attributes in the words. One does not think of oneself nor the Qur'ān recitation, nor the relation of divine gifts to the reciter, inasmuch as he or she would receive them; rather [the reciter] confines his or her care to the speaker, and concentrates all thought on Him as if engrossed in the vision of the speaker, apart from anything else.[5]

Denying all other thoughts, even of themselves, reciters can achieve a vision of God present at the recitation.

Of course, not all Muslims are mystics, nor can all recite the whole Qur'ān, though most memorize a few suras. Muslims can benefit from these direct experiences of God vicariously, however, through the stories of others. Therefore, the histories of great events and biographies of important mystics serve as signs of God's involvement in the world as much as the events themselves. By retelling pious stories, Muslims connect themselves to a tradition at least as old as the Qur'ān, which saw fit to remind believers of the story of Noah, his ark, and God's flood. So Muslims see God in the world around them, learn of God's plan through prophets and revelation, and have mystical visions of God. But all of these acts are tied up with memory, for a true Muslim is someone who remembers God's mercy and is thankful.

WHAT DO WE KNOW ABOUT GOD?

The Qur'ān offers a view of God which, at first glance, seems quite complete. God is, first and foremost, one. God shares power and position with no other being and nothing is like him.

Second, God is the all-powerful creator who determines all things in a perfectly ordered universe. Finally, God is merciful and just; he cares for creation and sustains it. These basic themes are found throughout the Qur'ān in both the Meccan and Medinan suras. From the very beginning of the Muslim community, however, doubts arose as to these basic premises. How could, for instance, God be pure unity, and yet be the source of a diverse creation? Or how could God determine all things and allow someone to commit a sin, but then judge that person to have sinned and damn him or her to hell? These questions are not answered in the Qur'ān, which, it seems, is quite comfortable maintaining the paradox. As the Muslim theological schools developed, however, questions about the nature of God eventually led to an inquisition (833–848) in which defenders of one view of God were tortured and killed. The question of what Muslims know about God is a serious one.

The first attempts to define God are found in the shorter suras of the Qur'ān. These are easily memorized, rhymed phrases that resemble creeds, or statements of faith. The first sura is one example.

> In the Name of God, the Merciful, the Compassionate.
> Praise belongs to God, the Lord of all Being,
> the All-merciful, the All-compassionate,
> the Master of the Day of Doom.
>
> Thee only we serve; to Thee alone we pray for succour.
> Guide us in the straight path,
> the path of those whom Thou hast blessed,
> not of those against whom Thou art wrathful,
> nor of those who are astray. (The Opening, 1:1–9)

This sura is usually recited five times a day, during the ritual prayer. It begins, like most suras, invoking God's name and his characteristic mercy and compassion. God is also described as both creator and judge of creation (the day of doom is that day when God will gather creation together and sit in judgment over it), but also as a refuge in time of need. In this way, God's roles at the beginning, middle, and end of time are delineated. Finally, God is described as granting both blessing and curse to creation. Noteworthy here is the imagery of staying on the path. For desert dwellers, finding the right path (the one to water and shelter, for instance) can mean the difference between life and death.

While this sura does not specifically assert that God is one, it does state that God is the source of good and evil, thereby ruling out dualistic systems, which seek to separate evil from God. Another short sura is more explicit:

> In the Name of God, the Merciful, the Compassionate.
> Say: "He is God, One,
> God, the Everlasting Refuge,
> who has not begotten, and has not been begotten,
> and equal to Him is not any one." (Sincere Religion, 112:1–4)

In Arabic, this sura is particularly beautiful: *qul: huwa -llāhu aḥad / Allāhu aṣ -ṣamad / lam yalid wa-lam yūlad / wa-lam yakun lahu kufūwan aḥad.* God's uniqueness is emphasized here through the imagery of giving birth—God is neither dependent on another being nor shares divine characteristics with another. But the idea of God having a child is more than mere imagery. Islam developed within a sectarian context; Mecca was the site of a central temple (the Ka'bah) devoted to a polytheistic cult; Medina had a substantial Jewish population; and both cities had Christian inhabitants. Moreover, the Arabs were traders who regularly traveled to Syria in the north and Yemen in the south. Although situated on the edge of these major civilizations, they were familiar with many religious practices.

God fathering a child, then, referred to both the Christian belief that Jesus was the son of God, and the local belief that the
god Allāh was the father of three daughters: al-Lāt, al-ʿUzzah,
and al-Manāt. The Qur'ānic idea of God is formulated in con-
tradistinction to the popular conception, first addressing the
"daughters of Allāh."

> Have you considered El-Lat and El-ʿUzza
>   and Manat the third, the other?
>   What, have you males, and He females?
>   That were indeed an unjust division.
>   They are naught but names yourselves have named, and your
> fathers; God has sent down no authority touching them. They
> follow only surmise, and what the souls desire; and yet guidance
> has come to them from their Lord. (The Star, 53:19–23)

This set of verses has been the source of much controversy since
the days of the earliest commentators, but what is important
for this discussion is the way the God of the Qur'ān is separated
from the popular belief of the Meccans. These verses also emphasize God's masculinity, and traditional Muslim texts always
refer to God as male. Separation from Christian beliefs was not
so easy, since the Qur'ān accepts the Gospel as God's word and
Jesus as a prophet; so Jesus cannot be dismissed as a mere
"name." In this case, the Qur'ān makes its point by recording a
dialogue between God and Jesus himself:

> And when God said, "O Jesus son of Mary, didst thou say unto
> men, 'Take me and my mother as gods, apart from God'?" [Jesus]
> said, "To Thee be glory! It is not mine to say what I have no right
> to. If I indeed said it, Thou knowest it, knowing what is in my
> soul, and I know not what is within Thy soul; Thou knowest the
> things unseen; I only said to them what Thou didst command
> me: 'Serve God, my Lord and your Lord.'" (The Table, 5:116)

If God's absolute monotheism was an idea that had to be insisted upon in the Qur'ān, God's characteristics of power and mercy were somewhat more familiar. The Arab audience to whom the Qur'ān was revealed was a believing one, depending on supernatural powers to sustain life in a harsh environment. A powerful and merciful god would have been attractive to them, although there remained much opposition to doctrines of resurrection and judgment day. The Qur'ān records some of these debates. For instance, one group is reported to hold the following views: "They say, 'There is nothing but our present life; we die, and we live, and nothing but Time (*dahr*) destroys us.'" To which God responds, "Of that they have no knowledge; they merely conjecture" (Hobbling, 45:23). This overwhelming fatalism is the same that can be seen in the work of pre-Islamic Arab poetry, where human frailty is contrasted with the cold, irresistible force of time. The use of the word *dahr* here, with its connotations of time, fate, and destiny, is particularly important. This fatalism and the word *dahr* drew direct fire from Qur'ānic exhortations. But it is important to note that the answering verse to the above reads: "Say, 'God gives you life then makes you die, then shall gather you to the Day of Resurrection, wherein there is no doubt, but most men do not know'" (Hobbling, 45:26). The Qur'ān does not merely replace old concepts of destiny with God, but sees God as a different kind of active principle in the world, as the author of life and death.

Muslim theologians had the difficult task of putting the Qur'ānic description of God into a logical framework. Their efforts were a serious attempt to answer the question, What can we know about God? For instance, does God decree that sinful acts should happen? On the one hand, if God does not make this decree, then something could occur without God's permission, but if God does make such a decree, then God is responsible for sin. An early creedal statement attempts to deal with this problem by removing God from evil, stating that sinful works are:

not in accordance with Allāh's commandment, yet in accordance
with His will; not in accordance with His desire, yet in accordance
with His decision; not in accordance with His good pleasure, yet
in accordance with His creation; not in accordance with His guidance; in accordance with His abandoning and His knowledge; yet
not in accordance with His intimate awareness or with His writing on the preserved tablet.[6]

A clear attempt is made here to deal with Qur'ānic language as
it describes God's action. By differentiating between God's
commandment and God's will, absolute power is maintained
(as God's will is all-pervasive), but also the essentially good nature of God (who cannot be seen as commanding an evil action) is affirmed. Furthermore, the last statement suggests an
attempt to understand the nature of the "preserved tablet" as
merely a description of events to come, not a determination of
individual sinful works.

The emphasis on God's role in this article of the creed seems
to suggest an early doctrine of *'adl,* God's essential justice. Because God is just, God could not command humanity to do
evil. However, the article also says that the faculty for originat-
ing an act occurs at the same time as the act. If this is true, then
there would be no time for the human actor to enter into the
decision of whether or not to commit that act. For example, say
God decreed that Ahmad should give 100 dollars to charity and
every act he undertakes, from writing the check to putting the
envelope in the mailbox, is predetermined by God. How, then,
is it right that Ahmad should get a heavenly reward for such an
action? A later theologian, al-Ash'arī (d. 935), recognized this
problem, but was unwilling to say that any action is undertaken
without God's command. Therefore, al-Ash'arī distinguished
between two types of events that take place in the human being.
The first occurs in us through God's act alone. This refers to
nonvoluntary actions, such as breathing and blinking. The sec-

ond type refers to conscious acts, which we do intentionally through an ability to act created in us at the moment the act occurs. At first glance, this seems similar to the above definitions, but a fine distinction is made in asserting that this ability does not include the ability to decide, but only an acquisition of the requisite power to perform the act, whether it is a good one or an evil one.

What al-Ash'arī is trying to do is give the human just enough power to have culpability for the act, but no more. Unlike previous thinkers, al-Ash'arī does not seem very concerned about associating God with evil, but rather puts the concept of good and evil—or justice—far above human understanding. But at the same time, his concept of God is by no means an arbitrary or cruel one. The following passage has been attributed to him:

> Allāh created the creatures free from unbelief and from belief. . . . Allāh did not compel any of His creatures to be infidels or faithful. And He did not create them either as faithful or infidels, but He created them as individuals, and faith and unbelief are the acts of men. . . . All the acts of men . . . are truly his own acquisition, but Allāh creates them.[7]

Further, he asserts: "Allāh guideth whomsoever He pleaseth, by grace, and He leadeth astray whomsoever He pleaseth, by justice."[8] Taken with the above doctrines, it is clear that God does work in terms of justice and grace, but that the meaning of these terms should not be deduced from human experience, but from God's action in the world. For some theologians, this was a satisfactory solution to the problem of determination and human action; al-Ash'arī seems to have tied up all the loose ends of his predecessors. The human being is neither a rival with God, sharing in God's creative power, nor merely a puppet in God's hands, fooled by an illusion of control. God's justice is maintained, as well as God's right to judge human beings based on their acts. Others did not agree, and allowed the human agent a greater role in deciding his or her own actions.

In reflecting on this debate, which raged for some three centuries, it is interesting to note the gradual progression to a more systematized and rational solution. The issues did not change radically, but the emphasis on creating a system did. Throughout, it was denied that God could act in a capricious or truly evil way. But by building a rational framework for understanding God's actions, the theologians seemed to be suggesting that God must conform to logic. Moreover, their very activity suggests that humans are capable of understanding God's action, though they are probably not able to do anything about it (unless God so wills). This is a rather audacious assertion, and it is not surprising that these theories were not widely understood or accepted.

Perhaps the most important part of this discussion, though, is the way it reveals a fundamental dichotomy in Islamic religious thought: the power of God versus necessary human action. This issue, first framed in the Qur'ān, commanded the interest of theologians from the earliest times. And while the discussions were certainly influenced by the old pre-Islamic concept of fate and destiny, it was finally God's determination of events that proved victorious. Even so, the human equation was not forgotten, and in this way, the Muslim theologians continued the debate begun three centuries earlier by the Qur'ān itself.

In trying to conceive of God, theologians were left with the basic problem of describing something that is unique ("equal to Him is not any one") in terms that humankind can understand. Any system, whether that of al-Ash'arī or someone else, tended to answer some questions by creating others. The Sufis also developed marvelous systems, based largely on Neoplatonic constructs, which explained God's relationship with creation. For the average Muslim, however, what was important was that God was just and all-powerful, demanding of all God's creatures worship and righteous living.

HOW DO WE RELATE TO GOD?
THE IMITATION OF GOD

Muslims do not imitate God's actions or characteristics, they obey God's commands. If the natural world was made for the enjoyment of humankind, then humankind was created to serve God. Therefore, one relates to God primarily through worship and divine service.

> I have not created jinn and mankind except to serve Me.
> I desire of them no provision, neither do I desire that they should feed me.
> Surely God is the All-provider, the Possessor of Strength, the Ever-sure. (The Scatterers, 51:56–58)

This is the fundamental truth of the creature's relationship to the creator, but upon this foundation, various systems of service have been erected. The most important of these systems is Islamic law, the *sharī'ah*. Islamic law orders every part of a believer's life, from prayer to marriage, defining what actions are acceptable to God. Since God is the creator and sustainer of the universe, the one who ordered all things, the believers' responsibility is to fit themselves into this order. This combination of rule and remembrance is found in the Qur'ān itself, particularly in the later Medinan suras.

> Today I have perfected your religion for you, and I have completed My blessing upon you, and I have approved Islam for your religion. But whosoever is constrained in emptiness and not inclining purposely to sin—God is All-forgiving, All-compassionate.
> They will question thee what is permitted them. Say: "The

good things are permitted you; and such hunting creatures as you teach, training them as hounds, and teaching them as God has taught you—eat what they seize for you, and mention God's Name over it. Fear God; God is swift at the reckoning."

Today the good things are permitted you, and the food of those who were given the Book is permitted to you and permitted to them is your food. Likewise believing women in wedlock, and in wedlock women of them who were given the Book before you if you give them their wages, in wedlock and not in license, or as taking lovers. Whoso disbelieves in the faith, his work has failed, and in the world to come he shall be among the losers.

O believers, when you stand up to pray wash your faces, and your hands up to the elbows, and wipe your heads, and your feet up to the ankles.

If you are defiled, purify yourselves; but if you are sick or on a journey, or if any of you comes from the privy, or you have touched women, and you can find no water, then have recourse to wholesome dust and wipe your faces and your hands with it. God does not desire to make any impediment for you; but He desires to purify you, and that He may complete His blessing upon you; haply you will be thankful.

And remember God's blessing upon you, and His compact which He made with you when you said, "We have heard and we obey." And fear you God; surely God knows the thoughts in the breasts. (The Table, 5:5–10)

Noteworthy in this passage is the way every rule is combined with an explanation of how fulfillment of the law effects a positive relationship with God. Twice the Qur'ān explains God's purpose in laying down rules as God's desire to "complete His blessing upon you." In a sense, human submission to God's law completes God's perfect creation. On the other hand, God does not wish for intricate rules on hunting techniques to become a burden for the believers, for law is not meant as an "impediment" for belief, but as a path leading to belief. The second of these verses even suggests that minor infractions against the law by a person who is "not inclining purposely to sin" can be forgiven.

The Qur'ān contains many rules and legal injunctions, some quite specific, such as the above directions for ritual purification, and some rather general. It is not, however, a legal handbook; nor does it seek to present a complete framework for legal speculation. First, Qur'ānic legislation is not grouped together; rather, it is interspersed throughout the text. In addition, only some 600 verses have any legal content at all, and of these, few concern strictly legal topics. Second, the Qur'ān makes no attempt to systematically cover all legal topics, though lists of rules are found in some suras (see suras 17 and 25, for instance). In other words, the Qur'ān is a modification of an already existing system and is dependent on the believer's ability to know God's command.

Over time, the basic requirements for the believer were condensed into "five pillars" of the Islamic faith. One of the first to formulate these pillars was al-Baghdādī (d. 1037), who asserted that the Prophet himself had said: "Five things are obligatory upon the children of Islam: testifying that there is no god but God, rising for the prayer, giving of charity, fasting in the month of Ramadan, and performing the pilgrimage to the house in Mecca."[9] All five of these practices can be seen as means of relating to God.

The testimony (*shahādah*) is the statement of faith said by every Muslim: "There is no god but God and Muḥammad is His prophet" (*lā ilāha illā -llāh wa-muḥammadu rasūlu -llāh*). The precise wording has varied over time and never appears in this form in the Qur'ān, though the Qur'ān certainly affirms the truth of the statement. Repeating this statement fulfills the obligation to remember God's bounty and mercy in sending the prophet Muḥammad to preach to humankind. The second pillar, ritual prayer (*ṣalāh*), plays a similar role. Five times a day, Muslims demonstrate their submission to God by making two or more full prostrations to God, touching their forehead to the ground. This prayer may be performed anywhere—home, office, or on the street—except for Friday noon, when Muslims gather at a mosque for communal prayer. Ritual prayer is the most visible manifestation of Islam, and the call to prayer is sung out, in Arabic, from mosques all over the world.

> God is most great, God is most great,
> God is most great, God is most great.
> I testify there is no god but God.
> I testify there is no god but God.
> I testify that Muḥammad is the prophet of God.
> I testify that Muḥammad is the prophet of God.
> Come to prayer, come to prayer;
> Come to prosperity, come to prosperity.
> God is most great, God is most great.
> I testify there is no god but God.

If prayer and testimony emphasize the obligations of the believers toward God, charity (*zakāh*) emphasizes the believers' obligations to their fellow Muslims, particularly the poor. There is no onus upon those who are wealthy in Islam; the Qur'ān clearly states that this world has been made for the purpose of enjoyment. But the wealthy do have an obligation to care for the poor, thereby fulfilling God's plan, or, in the words of the Qur'ān, "assaulting the steep."

> Have We not appointed to him two eyes,
> and a tongue, and two lips,
> and guided him on the two highways?
> Yet he has not assaulted the steep;
> and what shall teach thee what is the steep?

> The freeing of a slave,
> or giving food upon a day of hunger
> to an orphan near of kin
> or a needy man in misery;
> then that he become of those who believe
> and counsel each other to be steadfast,
> and counsel each other to be merciful.

Charity is institutionalized through an alms tax, bequests, and charitable foundations. Mosques, hospitals, and schools were traditionally funded through the generosity of the rich. And even today, many of the most popular medical clinics in Cairo are attached to mosques and paid for through private donations.

Fasting (*ṣawm*) in the month of Ramadan is also a clear reminder to believers of the poverty of others. From dawn till dusk for twenty-nine days every year, Muslims go without food, water, cigarettes, and sex to commemorate the revelation of the Qur'ān to the Prophet.

> O believers, prescribed for you is the Fast, even as it was prescribed for those that were before you—haply you will be godfearing—
>
> for days numbered; and if any of you be sick, or if he be on a journey, then a number of other days; and for those who are able to fast, a redemption by feeding a poor man. Yet better it is for him who volunteers good, and that you should fast is better for you, if you but know;
>
> the month of Ramadan, wherein the Koran was sent down to be a guidance to the people, and as clear signs of the Guidance and the Salvation. So let those of you, who are present at the month, fast it. (The Cow, 2:179–181)

The purpose of this fast is, in the words of the Qur'ān, to "magnify God that He has guided you" (2:181). By denying themselves the basic food and water needed to survive, believers are reminded of their absolute dependence on God. In most Muslim countries life slows down dramatically during Ramadan. Offices are often closed and many spend the day reading the Qur'ān, or taking long siestas to stave off hunger. Nightfall brings life to the cities once again, however. After the breaking of the fast at sunset, the streets fill with shoppers and shops reopen. Ramadan is also considered a time to remember God's mercy; shopkeepers set up tables on the street, inviting strangers to break the fast with them, and people make a special effort to see that no one goes hungry.

The final pillar is the pilgrimage (*ḥajj*) to Mecca. Unlike the other pillars, which had all been practiced in one form or another by the earliest community, the pilgrimage was instituted late in the Medinan period, after 630 C.E. The ritual is described in great detail in the Qur'ān, and every Muslim who can afford it is to undertake the pilgrimage at least once.

> The Pilgrimage is in months well-known; whoso undertakes the duty of Pilgrimage in them shall not go in to his womenfolk nor indulge in ungodliness and disputing in the Pilgrimage. Whatever good you do, God knows it. And take provision; but the best provision is godfearing, so fear you Me, men possessed of minds!
>
> It is no fault in you, that you should seek bounty from your Lord; but when you press on from Arafat, then remember God at the Holy Waymark, and remember Him as He has guided you, though formerly you were gone astray.
>
> Then press on from where the people press on, and pray for God's forgiveness; God is All-forgiving, All-compassionate. And when you have performed your holy rites remember God, as you remember your fathers or yet more devoutly. Now some men there are who say, "Our Lord, give to us in this world"; such men shall have no part in the world to come.
>
> And others there are who say, "Our Lord, give to us in this

world good, and good in the world to come, and guard us against
the chastisement of the Fire";
    those—they shall have a portion from what they have earned;
and God is swift at the reckoning. (The Cow, 2:193–98)

Today, millions journey to Mecca during the Muslim month of
Dhū l-Ḥijjah, traveling by boat, plane, and train and crying out
the ancient invocation *labayka!* to announce their presence to
God. They dress in simple white cloth, pray at the Kaʻbah (a
stone structure some forty feet high, said to have been built by
Abraham), and stand on the mountain of Arafat to "seek
bounty" from God. The entire ritual takes from two to four
days. By leaving their normal lives behind, dressing in purified
garments and traveling to a holy sanctuary at a particular time,
pilgrims enter God's space. For a brief moment, they leave the
world of human concerns and devote themselves entirely to
their spiritual relationship with God, asking for good "in this
world" and "good in the world to come."

For Muslims, God is an all-powerful deity who created the
world at the beginning of time, is constantly re-creating every
atom, and will gather the world and all human souls back to
God at the end of time. Through the Qur'ān and through
prophets, God makes himself known to all people, and, if humankind would just take a moment to reflect, they would see
that his creation bears witness to him.

Have you considered the water you drink?
Did you sent it down from the clouds, or did We send it?
Did We will, We would make it bitter; so why are you not
thankful?

Have you considered the fire you kindle?
Did you make its timber to grow, or did We make it?

We Ourselves made it for a reminder, and a boon to the desert-
dwellers. (The Terror, 56:67–72)

God has ninety-nine most beautiful names, each describing an
attribute: the All-Knowing, the Almighty, the All-Seeing. But
these all come down to three main characteristics of God,
which are justice, power, and mercy. How does one relate to
such an overwhelming deity, who can barely be conceived of by
limited human intelligence? One starts with humility and worship as defined by the tenets of Islamic law, and then continues
to remember God's bounty in every act of life.

It is He who made the earth submissive to you; therefore walk in
its tracts, and eat of His provision; to Him is the Uprising. (The
Kingdom, 67:15)

CHAPTER 5

Christianity

HOW DO WE KNOW ABOUT GOD?

O r, for that matter: how do we know about anyone? What
happens, such that I can say I "know" another person? Of
my many social encounters every day, relatively few of them
will involve people I "know," and that means that our knowledge of people must be more than a matter of just putting a
name to them. So it is with God. I "know" God, not merely because I am willing to say that the creator of the universe is
something or someone called God, and not merely because a
certain proposition about God convinces me in intellectual
terms. As a Christian, I know God as a matter of personal familiarity, as I would know a person.

Christianity typically and persistently interprets the knowledge of God in terms of our knowledge of persons. St. Paul
provides a fine example. When he describes his own conversion, he does not refer to external phenomena, although the
story as given by St. Luke in Acts, chapters 9 and 22, does involve supernatural occurrences. But Paul himself simply speaks
of the moment when "it pleased God—who had separated me
from my mother's womb and called me through his grace—to
reveal his Son in me" (Gal. 1:15–16, written around the year 53
c.e.). That direct statement is a vivid, existential description,
and at the same time a normative account of how Christians
know God personally. God creates us, calls us, and provides

the image of God's own humanity—God's Son—within us. That is the basis of our knowledge of God, rather than an understanding of propositions; knowing God as the one, and the only One, who creates and calls and shapes us is our special knowledge of God.

Knowledge of God within Christianity is not first of all a matter of what we can say about God, but a function of personal familiarity with God and trust in God. St. Paul's statement needs some explanation in order for us to see the kind of personal familiarity with God he had in mind. Fortunately, he himself provides very clear indications of how he sees us as created, called, and shaped within ourselves by God, and by following his explanations we can understand how Christianity conceives of our knowledge about God. In following St. Paul and the other theologians mentioned here, God is conceived of personally, and therefore (given conventions in Greek and Latin) in terms of what "he" does with "his" creation, and how that creation approaches "him." We will simply follow that usage in the present case; the volume on "Women" will permit us to open the question of a sexually inclusive conception of God in Christianity.

St. Paul wrote very extensively to a Christian community in Rome around 57 C.E.(four years after he wrote to the Galatians in Asia Minor). His letter to the Romans is the result, the fullest available explanation of Paul's theology. In an opening section, Paul concerns himself with the issue of how God may be conceived of as judging people, when they do not know God. His response is that God's power and divinity are primordially evident to people from the world around them:

> What is known of God is evident to them, because God has manifested it to them. His invisible qualities, his eternal power and divinity, have been demonstrated perceptibly from the creation of the world by the things that have been made. (Rom. 1:19–20)

The issue of judgment, which is the context of Paul's statement, will not concern us here, because that topic is taken up in the volume on "Afterlife." Our present concern is with how Paul understands God to be known to humanity at large. To Paul the particular qualities of God, because they are behind the world rather than in it, are invisible. God's being God means that God is transcendent in divinity, beyond the terms of reference of time and space. But God's power is also evident, demonstrated by our perception of things made in the world around us.

The world is not just an accident of our environment, but that which is created by God. Paul's conviction is consonant with the story of the creation in Genesis 1, and with much else in the Old Testament. Sometimes, the joyful expression that we live in a divine creation approaches romanticism. In 1712, Joseph Addison in England wrote a paraphrase of Psalm 19, which was subsequently set to music written by Franz Josef Haydn, and the hymn is still used in many churches:

> The spacious firmament on high,
> With all the blue ethereal sky,
> And spangled heavens, a shining frame,
> Their great Original proclaim.
> The unwearied sun from day to day
> Does his Creator's power display;
> And publishes to every land
> The work of an almighty hand.

Addison's paraphrase is typical of the English Enlightenment in its stress upon the regular pattern of creation in its relation to the recognition of God.

In fact, the final stanza of Addison's paraphrase makes it clear beyond a doubt that, for him, the existence of God is an inference of reason:

What though in solemn silence all
Move round the dark terrestrial ball?
What though no real voice nor sound
Amid their radiant orbs be found?
In reason's ear they all rejoice,
And utter forth a glorious voice;
For ever singing as they shine,
"The hand that made us is divine."

Writing in a period in which the angels in heaven were being steadily replaced by laws of nature, Addison paraphrased the psalm along the lines of the Pauline insight: The natural world attests the invisible power and transcendence of God.

Of course, Paul did not limit his claim to the inferences of reason. He concluded that what could be known of God was "evident," a more immediate matter of perception, rather than reasoned argument. But Addison clearly pursued Paul's insight in a new key, and also provided it with an almost romantic sense of delight in nature (a sense that Haydn's music reinforces).

When Paul refers to God separating him from his mother's womb in Galatians 1:15, there is nothing abstract or theoretical about the imagery of creation. The emphasis rather falls on the immediate and personal link between God and Paul's own being. The imagery is not original with Paul: he is picking up the language of the Old Testament, for example in the book of Psalms. Psalm 22:9 and Psalm 71:6 offer praise to God for taking the speaker from the womb and keeping him safe from childhood. The image is also used in the prophetic literature, when the prophet is said to have been taken from the womb for the purpose of giving his prophecy (see Isaiah 49:1 and Jeremiah 1:5). In all these cases, as in Paul's usage, the imagery expresses not only a sense of being in an ordered creation, but of experiencing God's care within that creation. The prophetic usage enhances the emphasis on one's personal sense of purpose by applying the image to a particular mission one is to accomplish. Paul shares that emphasis, as well.

The prophetic dimension of Paul's reference to God comes out again in his description of God "calling" him in Galatians 1:15. The motif that God "calls" is so widespread in the biblical tradition, its significance might easily be overlooked. The basic meaning of the motif is expressed in the story of the prophet Samuel's call (1 Samuel 3:1–14). The boy Samuel is staying with the priest Eli, attending the ark and its sacrificial worship. It was a time when "the word of the Lord" and vision were rare. But when Samuel slept at night near the ark, God called to him so clearly, Samuel thought it was Eli calling him. Three times he went to Eli, to ask what he wanted, and Eli finally instructed him to answer, "Speak, Lord, for thy servant hears." The result is that God begins to tell Samuel what God is about to do. Samuel commences his prophetic ministry, which leads to the anointing of David as king of Israel.

"Calling," then, is understood to establish a link between God and the person called, so that God's word may be delivered. Who is called? It might be a prophet, or all Israel, or Jesus himself. Matthew 2:15 presents the infant Jesus as called from Egypt for his vocation in Israel, in citing the prophetic book of Hosea (11:1). "Out of Egypt I called my Son" is applied by Hosea to the people Israel, liberated at the time of the Exodus. That wording is then interpreted afresh in Matthew to refer to Jesus. That is possible because much of the language of the Old Testament, including reference to God's calling and God's separating a person from the womb, is deliberately developed in the New Testament. The usage of the Old Testament is the point of departure for new applications and unusual developments, designed to convey a sense of intimacy with God.

God initiates the biblical call, but the call must be answered for it to be productive of the communication that is the purpose of the calling. Indeed, the fact of God's call can be the basis on which people take it upon themselves to call upon God. "Answer me when I call, O God of my righteousness" (Psalm 4:1) is an appeal that is predicated on the previous response to God's call on the part of the psalmist and the psalmist's community.

The reciprocity of call and response is particularly developed by Paul in his teaching in regard to the Spirit of God. 1 Corinthians 2 shows how, in a letter written a year or two before Romans, Paul sees Spirit at work. If one asks how we can know what God has prepared for us, the answer is that Spirit alone is able to communicate divine purposes.

Paul develops his position by quoting a passage from Isaiah 64:4 (in 1 Cor. 2:9), which speaks of things beyond human understanding that God has readied for those who love him, and Paul then goes on to say:

> God has revealed them to us through the Spirit; for the Spirit searches all things, even the depths of God. For who among men knows the things of man except the spirit of man which is in him? So also no one has known the things of God except the Spirit of God. (1 Cor. 2:10–11)

As Paul sees human relations, one person can only know what another thinks and feels on the basis of their shared "spirit." "Spirit" is the name for what links one person with another, and by means of that link we can also know what God thinks and feels. The Spirit at issue in knowing God, Paul goes on to say, is not "the spirit of the world," but "the Spirit which is of God" (1 Cor. 2:12). The human spirit, which is the medium of ordinary human exchange, becomes as the result of God's effective calling the vehicle of divine revelation.

Paul's remark in 1 Corinthians 2 is part of a complete anthropology, which is spelled out further in 1 Corinthians 15, his classic explanation of what resurrection involves. When Paul thinks of a person, he conceives of a body as composed of flesh. Flesh in his definition is physical substance, which varies from one created thing to another (for example, people, animals, birds, and fish; 1 Cor. 15:39). But in addition to being physical bodies, people are also what Paul calls a "psychic body," by which he means bodies with souls (1 Cor. 15:44). (Unfortunately, the phrase is wrongly translated in many modern versions, but its dependence on the noun for "soul" [*psukhe*] shows what the real sense is.) In other words, people as bodies are not just lumps of flesh, but they are self-aware. That self-awareness is precisely what makes them "psychic body."

Now in addition to being physical body and psychic body, Paul says we are or can become "spiritual body" (1 Cor. 15:44). That is, we can relate thoughts and feelings *to one another and to God,* as 1 Corinthians 2 has already shown us. Jesus is therefore the last Adam, a "life-giving spirit" (1 Cor. 15:45) just as the first Adam was a "living being" or "soul" (the two words are the same in Greek, *psukhe*). Jesus is the basis on which we can realize our identities as God's children, the brothers and sisters of Christ, and know the power of the resurrection. (A discussion of what that means for people must, again, be deferred until the volume on "Afterlife"; the present concern is with Jesus as the source of Spirit.) In presenting Jesus in this way, Paul defines a distinctive Christology as well as a characteristic spirituality.

The initial terms of Paul's knowledge of God, then, are his awareness of God's power and care, and his access to the Spirit of God. But that is by no means the whole of Paul's knowledge of God. Its distinctive feature is that God was pleased "to reveal his Son in me" (Gal. 1:16): that is how Paul knows in the first place that he has been separated from the womb and called by God. The revelation of God's Son in the midst of one's being is the distinctive basis of Christian knowledge of God. In fact, Paul conceives of the moment of receiving God's Spirit in a highly specific manner, linked inextricably to Jesus (Gal. 4:6):

Because you are sons, God sent the Spirit of his Son into our hearts, crying, Abba—Father.

Baptism is the moment at which, by accepting the revelation of the Son, one can accept that Spirit which is truly divine. Only what has come from God can acknowledge and respond to God: that is the revelation of God's Son within.

Paul brings us, then, to the most characteristic aspect of the Christian understanding of the knowledge of God—its emphasis upon Jesus, the Son of God, as the central mediator of that knowledge. One's own acknowledgment of and response to God remain vital, but they are understood to be possible only because God has already been at work within, shaping a spiritual eye to see God at work and a spiritual ear to hear God's call. As Paul conceives of Jesus, he is first of all the Son of God revealed within us. Of course, Paul is aware of the primitive teaching concerning Jesus' deeds and teaching, including a graphic account of his crucifixion (see Galatians 3:1). But his interest in Jesus is not historical. Rather, his attention is taken up by how the revelation of the Son of God might shape our minds and hearts to know God.

The most famous expression of this theme occurs in the letter to the Philippians, which was probably composed after Paul's death by his follower Timothy (c. 90 C.E.). It represents a mature Pauline theology, much of it on the basis of what Paul personally had thought. It was composed at a time at which Christians in the Greco-Roman world were largely of the servant class, so that its appeal to the form of Jesus as a servant is especially poignant (Phil. 2:5–8):

Let this thought prevail among you, which was also in Christ Jesus: Who, being in God's form, did not consider the presumption of equality with God, but emptied himself, taking a servant's form; existing in men's likeness, and found as a man in shape, he humbled himself, becoming obedient unto death, death on a cross.

The point of Paul and Timothy together (see Philippians 1:1) is that it is possible, on the basis of the revelation of the Son of God within one, to think as Jesus did, although in one's own circumstances. Here is an example of the imperative to imitate Christ within the New Testament. Its object is not a slavish mimicry of the historical person, but an embrace of that humble disposition of Christ that makes the knowledge of God possible, proceeding as it does from God's own loving nature.

Knowledge of God, then, involves the capacity to acknowledge God as the source of one's being, the ability to respond to God's call and to hear God, and an acceptance within oneself of Christ's own loving disposition, his humility unto death. How, then, do we know God? By discovering and reshaping who we truly are in the image of God's Son.

WHAT DO WE KNOW ABOUT GOD?

Once we appreciate *how* we know God, it is easy to see why in Christianity God is principally known as Father, Son, and Spirit. Those are God's aspects as God creates us, provides the image of God's humanity within us, and calls us. That God is to be known as the Trinity may seem to be a confusing statement, because it can be mistaken for an assertion that there are three Gods. Christianity avoids any such claim, and insists that it is speaking of the one God. At the same time, the Trinity is held to express how God relates both internally, within God's own being, and externally, to humanity. In terms of the confusions that are possible today—and in terms of its historical development—the teaching of the Trinity is best approached by beginning with the Son in relation to the Father. The place of the Holy Spirit is more easily determined once the fundamental question of Christology has been dealt with.

The passage from Philippians that has just been considered closes its praise of Jesus' example with a conclusion that sets out that praise in the clearest possible terms:

So that at the name of Jesus every knee should bow, in heaven and
on earth and within the depths, and every tongue acknowledge
that Jesus Christ is Lord, to the glory of God, the Father. (Phil.
2:10–11)

There is no mistaking the imagery of every knee bowing and
every tongue acknowledging Jesus as Sovereign: God himself
says in Isaiah 45:23, "To me every knee shall bow, every tongue
shall swear." Paul and Timothy are applying that prophecy to
Jesus, and putting him in the position of God.

In the interpretation of the classic theologian of the Trinity,
St. Augustine, the passage from Philippians revealed a fundamental truth about God. Augustine (354–430) was bishop of
Hippo in North Africa. Born in North Africa of humble origins, Augustine had made his way as a professor of rhetoric until his conversion to Christianity while he was in Milan. From
there he returned to North Africa, and was leading a life of
philosophical leisure until he was called to Hippo for ordina-
tion to the priesthood, and eventually service as bishop. His
treatise *On the Trinity*, some twenty years in the making (from
400 C.E.), represents the intellectual climax of his career. The
central problem that he wrestled with for years before and after
his conversion was that of the nature of God. For Augustine,
the divine nature, or essence, was precisely what the Trinity
concerned.

In Philippians 2:6–7, Christ is praised because he "did not
consider the presumption of equality with God, but emptied
himself, taking a servant's form." That can only be said, according to Augustine, because the Son existed *prior* to becoming
flesh, and freely chose the form of servanthood. He did not
consider taking equality with God, but he might have done so.
After all, he was "in God's form" when he decided instead to become a servant, the only mortal form he ever took (*On the Trinity* I.11, 13; II.11). *The Son was an eternal aspect of God's being*

before being known as the man Jesus Christ. By becoming human
and taking on the form of a servant, he permitted those who
were willing to become servants of others after him to discover
the way of God on earth.

The implications for understanding Christ are evident, and
Augustine does not hesitate to spell them out:

> Even then, when the Lord was born of a virgin . . . it was not the
> Word of God in his own substance, by which he is equal and co-
> eternal to the Father . . . but assuredly a creature . . . which could
> appear to bodily and mortal senses. (*On the Trinity* III.11)

Here Augustine provides the key to a Christian evaluation of Jesus. He is a mortal person, a "creature" within natural conditions and historical time, and he can be understood as such.
But just this person also embodies God's "Word," the divine
plan for all time. That "Word" was revealed to the prophets of
Israel according to their own perception of it, but in the case of
Jesus that "Word"—God's own loving design for humanity—
actually became flesh. For that reason, all that has been accu-
rately said in the Old Testament may be said to be fulfilled in
the New Testament. In his association of Christ with the
prophetic Word of God, Augustine reflects a tradition of
thought that reaches back to the opening of the Gospel according to John (see John 1:1–18). But he is more acute than most
Christian thinkers in his distinction between the created person
called Jesus and the eternal Son who is the Father's equal.

God, then, creates us as Father and redeems us as Son. Likewise, God as Holy Spirit communicates God's unique essence;
Spirit is God's self-giving (*On the Trinity* V.11–16). Augustine
acknowledges that there is no established vocabulary that can
convey the meaning of the Trinity. He is familiar with the reference to "essence" and "nature" among some Greek theologians,
to whom we will refer in a moment. He admits that, to refer to

what unifies the Trinity, "essence" (*ousia*, in Greek) is better than the common Latin term "substance" (*substantia*) (*On the Trinity* V.2–4, see also VII.4–5). His worry about "substance" is that its meaning might be confused with material composition. But whether seen as unique essence or unique substance, Father, Son, and Spirit are to be understood as the exalted Trinity, in which each is God, but there are not three Gods (*On the Trinity* V.8). That is so because they are all aspects of a single and unique essence, the substance of divinity alone.

Augustine's Greek predecessors in the exposition of the Trinity are known as the Cappadocian Fathers (St. Basil, St. Gregory of Nazianzus, St. Gregory of Nyssa), from the region of Asia Minor in which they were active during the fourth century. The Cappadocian Fathers borrowed from the vocabulary of Greek philosophy in order to explain the relationships among Father, Son, and Spirit. The statement of faith called the Nicene Creed had already established the Son as being "of one substance" (*ousia* in Greek, *substantia* in Latin) with the Father, but how could the differences within the Trinity be expressed? The Cappadocians used the term "nature" (*hypostasis* in Greek), so that they spoke of one essence and three natures. But Augustine, along with many Latin Christians, complained that the term "nature" seemed pretty much the same as "essence," and in fact both of them could be translated by the Latin term "substance."

For that reason, Augustine accepted the Latin practice of speaking of the Trinity as three "persons" in one "substance," rather than of three "natures" in one "essence." But he warned his readers that the words used have no authority in themselves; we only use them "in order that we might not be obliged to remain silent" (*On the Trinity* V.9). Despite such warnings, however, different uses of language to explore the Trinity have caused a deep rift between what came to be called the Orthodox Church in the East and what came to be called the Catholic Church in the West.

Knowledge of the Trinity must obviously be beyond words because words emerge from the terms and relations of this world, not directly from God. When Augustine tried to explore the true nature of God, he found that the best possible medium would be to analyze love. After all, God is love (so 1 John 4:7–10) and God commands love (so Mark 12:28–34 and parallels); it must be that love is the gift of God within us, so we must understand love in order to know God. In general terms, we can even say that the Trinity is reflected in the relationship between the lover, the beloved, and love itself (*On the Trinity* VIII.7–IX.2).

Augustine's emphasis on the interior gift of love led him to turn away from exterior relations among people (which the Cappadocian Fathers had in any case explored) and to seek the truth of love within the human mind. There, his favorite analogy to the Trinity was that a mind is possessed of memory, understanding, and will, and these are not "three minds, but one mind":

> For I remember that I have memory, understanding, and will; and I understand that I understand, will, and remember; and I will that I will, remember, and understand. (*On the Trinity* X.11–12)

Augustine's analogy of a single human mind has led to the accusation that the differences among the Trinity are minimized. On the other hand, the Cappadocians' analogy of three people living in a village had led to the accusation that their picture of the Trinity was practically of three Gods. In the climate of controversy during the fourth and fifth centuries, it is doubtful that *any* analogy of the Trinity, no matter how nuanced, could have avoided causing offense in some quarter or another.

But the fundamental insight that animates the work of the Cappadocians and Augustine alike is that the one God is known to us in three aspects, and that God is related internally in those aspects. The Trinity is not just a way of knowing God, but an account of how God is. Creativity, redemption, communication—these are all essential and distinct aspects of God's being God.

If we wish to convert the Cappadocian and Augustinian analogies into a fresh perspective, we might return to our reflection on how we come to know another human being. Among all the people I can name, I might come to know and to love a person as I become familiar with her or him.

A person, as distinct from the multitude of people whom I might know (but do not), reveals particular intentions and purposes as I get to know him or her. These intentions are associated with a particular personality and character. And both the intentions and the personality become familiar to me because the person communicates, shares herself or himself. A useful analogy of the Trinity, then, is how we know another person as a person; the image of God in creation (Gen. 1:27) is the best image of God in theological reflection, provided it is considered in the perspective of love.

HOW DO WE RELATE TO GOD? THE IMITATION OF GOD

Just as love is the principle within our experience that enables us to know God, so it is the basis of our coming into a direct and redeeming relationship with God. The passage in 1 John that says that God is love is worth citing at some length, to see to what extent loving is held to be a principle of comprehensive transformation:

> Beloved, we ought to love one another, because love is from God, and everyone who loves has been begotten from God and knows God. He who does not love does not know God, because God is love. By this has the love of God been made evident among us, that God sent his only begotten Son into the world, that we might live through him. (1 John 4:7–9)

God's creation of the world in love, the purpose and power of the Father, corresponds to a fully human character—the personality of the Son. For that reason, the imperative to love as God loves us is also a call to follow the example of the Son.

The connection between loving as God loves and following the example of the Son is explicitly made in 1 John:

> In this we know love, that he laid down his life for us, and we ought to lay down our lives for the brethren. (1 John 3:16)

The call to realize the symmetry between Christ and the believer, which is usually known as "the imitation of Christ" (*imitatio Christi*), is a perennial theme of Christian ethics, and the most characteristic theme. The reason for that emphasis is that Jesus provides the model and the reality of God in human form. Imitating him is at one and the same time the imitation of God.

Once the *imitatio Christi* is understood in this fashion, two otherwise puzzling and persistent features of Christian theology become explicable. First, curiosity about Jesus in his personality—in the modern period, "the historical Jesus"—is by no means a purely speculative concern. The moving force of that curiosity is a desire to understand the life that, by imitation, transforms our lives into the likeness of God. Second, because imitating Jesus is imitating God, it is perfectly natural for Christians to wonder in what precise ways Jesus' divinity was evident during his lifetime. Those two issues—Jesus in his actual life and Jesus in relation to the Father and the Spirit—are profoundly Trinitarian, and have been prominent in every major epoch of Christian thought and life. Expressions of the two concerns are enormously varied; the concerns in themselves are consistent.

The crux of Christian life, however, is not speculative. Whatever one might think of God, the purpose of life, as Gregory of Nyssa put the matter, is to imitate God through Christ and to be transformed into an eternal child of God on that basis. (See his elegant letter, *On What Is Meant by the Profession "Christian."*) For all that it is intellectually stimulating, the Trinity's proper function is to arouse the sort of active love that is at its source. That is possible principally because, in addition to our being created by God and provided with the Son's love as an example, love is communicated to us by means of the Holy Spirit.

The ways in which the Holy Spirit is experienced are, to say the least, varied within Christian tradition. Within the modern period, the Quaker discipline of waiting upon what are usually called "movings" of the Spirit provides many examples. Perhaps the most accessible is that of John Woolman (1720–1772), who left a detailed diary of his personal understanding of what was happening to him. He did not begin his diary until he was thirty-six years old, and speaks in retrospect of a gradually growing seriousness of reflection and an intentional quietness in his life. The result was he learned to speak "under a strong exercise of spirit":

> My understanding became more strengthened to distinguish the language of the pure Spirit which inwardly moves upon the heart . . . until I felt that rise which prepares the creature to stand like a trumpet through which the Lord speaks to his flock.

Within the social history of the United States, Woolman's influence extended far beyond his personal practice and the Quaker meetings he began to address.

He refused to draw up bills of sale for slaves, as required by his employer in Philadelphia. In addition to resisting slavery, he opposed paying taxes for war and accepting payment for quartering troops. He advocated fair wages and working hours, affordable education, and a "reformation" of society on the basis of nonviolent confrontation. When he considered making one of his many tours to oppose the practice of slavery, Woolman had an actual vision:

> As I opened my eyes I saw a light in my chamber at the apparent distance of five feet, about nine inches diameter, of a clear, easy brightness and near the center the most radiant. As I lay still without any surprise looking upon it, words were spoken to my inward ear which filled my whole inward man. They were not the effect of thought nor any conclusion in relation to the appearance, but as the language of the Holy One spoken in my mind.

Such experiences punctuate Woolman's diary, and drove him to extraordinary lengths. Despite a recent bout with pleurisy, he traveled to England in 1772. (Moreover, he traveled in steerage to share the conditions of young seamen.) He wished to speak out for the poor in the North and to influence the London Yearly Meeting of Quakers against the slave trade. After extensive travels in England following that successful Meeting, Woolman died in York of smallpox.

Woolman's diary makes it plain that experience of the Holy Spirit may not be understood as a single, aberrant event. The visions that punctuate his diary occur within a regular practice of reading the Scriptures (and much else). His reflection on God as creator led him to see justice toward all creatures as an imperative. His experience of "the love of God through Jesus Christ to redeem me" awakened compassion within him. Woolman's reflective practice and rational consideration, as well as his political judgments, were involved within a meditative focus on God as Creator, Redeemer, and Sanctifier.

That has been the typical pattern of Christian experience of God, which is essentially Trinitarian. As such, it is understood to derive from God's Self, communicating as Spirit to our spirits. What is discovered when we encounter God, then, is not a definition of what divinity is. Rather, God's essence is such that it awakens a realization of who we are, and on that basis we can become familiar with God. The One who makes us human also loves us and reveals the divine Self to us. It is God's very nature to be making and loving and revealing. That is why we are called to become new selves—God's children in the imitation of Christ. And that is why, only in becoming what we are in our truest selves (the selves that God has given), can we come to know God.

Literary Sources of the World's Religions
1. *The Koran Interpreted* (New York: Macmillan, 1955).
2. For example, a version of the Chinese Buddhist canon, published in Tokyo in the 1920s, is made up of fifty-five Western-style volumes totaling 2148 texts!

Introduction
1. Melford E. Spiro, "Religion: Problems of Definition and Explanation," in *Culture and Human Nature: Theoretical Papers of Melford E. Spiro*, ed. Benjamin Kilbourne and L. L. Langness (Chicago: University of Chicago Press, 1987), 187–222.

2. Hinduism
1. Translated by Vasudha Narayanan, in *The Tamil Veda: Revelation, Recitation, and Ritual* (Columbia: University of South Carolina Press, 1994), 78. Used by permission of the translator.
2. Ibid., 168.

3. Buddhism
1. *Dīgha Nikāya* I.222–23.
2. *The Experience of Buddhism*, trans. John S. Strong (Belmont, Calif.: Wadsworth, 1995), 154–55.
3. Donald S. Lopez Jr., ed., *Buddhism in Practice*, quote trans. Daniel B. Stevenson (Princeton, N.J.: Princeton University Press, 1995), 375–76.
4. Ibid., quote trans. Luis O. Gomez, 325–27.

4. Islam

1. Fazlur Rahman, *Major Themes of the Qur'ān,* 2d ed. (Minneapolis: Bibliotheca Islamica, 1989), 68.
2. Al-Ghazzālī, *Ihyā 'Ulūm al-Dīn* (Beirut: Dār al-Fikr, 1991), vol. 1, 331.
3. Ibid., 332.
4. Ibid., 339.
5. Ibid.
6. A. J. Wensinck, *The Muslim Creed* (Cambridge: Cambridge University Press, 1932), 126.
7. Ibid., 191.
8. Ibid., 195.
9. Al-Baghdādī, *Kitāb Usūl al-Dīn,* quoted in Rippin and Knappert, *Textual Sources for the Study of Islam* (Chicago: University of Chicago Press, reprint ed. 1990), 89.